AS THE JOURNEY
BEGINS

GEORGE MILLS

ISBN: 979-8-88945-364-2 (paperback)
eISBN: 979-8-88945-365-9

Brilliant Books Literary
137 Forest Park Lane Thomasville
North Carolina 27360 USA

Printed in the United States of America

This book is not directly intended to any person whatso-ever. I'm just telling it as I see it being in my life journey.

First and foremost, I shall give thanks to the Lord my God for giving me the ability to use my imagination to be writing this little book. I would like to dedicate this book to all who has inspired me to continue write it. I have always loved to write poems, so one day on my lunch break, I decided to put my thoughts into words. I asked a friend, "Just how does this sound to you?"

My friend replied, "You came up with this? It sounds great. You have a great imagination. You might need to keep this up."

So I decided to just see where I could go with it from there, and that is how this book came about. May you find it interesting to read.

AS THE JOURNEY BEGINS

As I start this second day of this journey we call life, I have dis-covered as a free, single man who has put God first in his life, that finding a good-hearted woman who seeks God first in her life and who is willing to put the needs of her family first and foremost is hard to find. They are few and far between as it stands for now. Some women nowadays are just out to play games, and some women have no clue as to what they want in life. They are like a diamond in the rough whose rough edges God is still smoothing. And so the search continues as I slowly travel down this ole rugged road that we call life. Be sure to check in tomorrow for any further updates, if any.

On the third day of this journey called life, I start down this ole rugged road once again. I find that there are some women who like to just use you for a time to satisfy their needs and then leave you hanging out to dry knowing not what you have done wrong, or even if you had done anything wrong, or where to go next.

As the journey on the fourth day begins. I gain insight on how some women are indecisive. At times in their lives, they are unwilling to take the initiative, to take the opportunity placed before them to find out if a relationship would flourish or not. As we both know there's no stings are attach that give no lasting strong background for a relationship which that may blossom or become an everlasting rela-tionship as time goes by. Could it be as time truly goes on down this ole rugged road that we may find out she has not truly founded her way in life, or could it be that life has thrown her into a tailspin that she has not yet come out of, not to say she has not found her way in life. She just has not been truly treated as a woman should be treated, as one who could make a beautiful helpmate for the man that needs her, so they remain one that our Heavenly Father has joined together. So the journey continues. I travel slowly down this ole rugged road that we call life in search of that helpmate that God has created for that man, knowing for sure that God has created her for him, for in the beginning of time God put Adam to sleep to take a rib from him to create a helpmate for him. Therefore, he knows she is somewhere out there in this world, all alone, in search of that man herself. She was treated the way she was in the past by a man who is unworthy of her love and was just out to used her for a time for his pleasure, leaving her to fend for herself, leaving her in uncertainty, unable to ever truly trust in a man; therefore, she has tried to make it on her own for so long and is now afraid to take the opportunity that is put before her.

As the fifth day of this journey starts down this ole rugged road of what we might call life, I find that there are some women who are stuck-up. They are just stuck on their selves, thinking that they may be better then you, or could it be that they may be thinking that you are better than them, but only time will tell as I continue this life journey down this ole rugged road filled with hills and curves, ditches and valleys.

On the sixth day down this road, I came to discover something by just talking to other men along the way; they suggested that one should test drive the vehicle before you take it off the car lot. Well, I am not the type of man who would treat a woman in that way. That's the very reason she has been thrown into a tailspin from the get-go. That is not the way I think God intended for it to be done. He put Adam to sleep to take a rib from him to create a beautiful woman for his helpmate, not to be used and abused by him but to be loved and cherished her as a woman should be. She is not for his pleasure alone; should he not take into consideration her feeling and needs as well? Her being the weaker vessel of the two of them. After all, is she not a part of your own flesh in which God created her from? Would you not want to treat her with the same respect that you would want her to treat you with?

As I start this seventh day of this journey down this ole rugged road, I come to a fork in the road and discovered this question: why should a woman spend a lifetime waiting on a man to change his ways? If she is waiting on a man to change, then apparently she is waiting on the wrong thing. I must say that she has not truly dis-covered who she is in her walk with God, for God will put the right man who he has changed for her in her path at the right time, but before he can do just that, she must first find her true faith in her walk with God. Then and only then can God put the right man in her life. Likewise, the man must have true faith in his walk with God himself; otherwise, the relationship between both will not flourish into an everlasting, beautiful relationship. God created them both to enjoy each other's company as they start their journey together as one down this ole rugged road.

COUNTRY BOY VOCABULARY

The eighth day of this journey continues in life, only to find as I stop and put some thought into this journey over the past seven days, I find myself as a person who can only express himself by put-ting his thoughts down on paper. By doing this I find myself to be more at ease in explaining the true way I feel about certain things. I ask a friend to read what I have written so for in this journey. He explains that it is as if I had a revelation in my life, to what went wrong in my life. I started to reflect back over the past year to what I think may have gone wrong. It is that I took my eyes off God and his way when I should be living my life while putting him first and foremost. I put my needs and hers first and foremost. I put our needs first and foremost and forgot that God has created us both to be as one to serve and obey his request.

We should not think of putting our own needs first and fore-most in our own life, but be more obedient to God and his request. After all, is it not God who created us all in his own image from the beginning of time? Hasn't he been the sole provider in all our needs in this journey of life that God has created? So with that being said, I say to you all, just be more obedient to God's request, and he will provide all your needs as you journey on down this ole rugged road that we call life. Until you accept him as your personal savior, you will have trials and tribulations like you have never had in your life.

I am not trying to say that once you have accepted God as your personal savior that your will not have trial and tribulations, but as you journey down this ole rugged road that we call life, your trials and tribulations will become much easier for you to deal.

Ninth day of this journey, I find it easier in some certain situations to express my thoughts to other people without feeling nervous around them about what I must say. Could it be that I have come to realize that I should have put God first in my life, therefore making my own trials and tribulation much easier for me to deal with? I continue in what may be one of the hardest journey one could find himself on in search of a lovely soul mate, who I do believe that God has created for me from the beginning of time. As it stands for now, I have not met a lovely lady as the one I have described as in the beginning of my journey. Could it be that I have been looking in all the wrong places? Or could it be that it is not in God's plans for me to meet her just yet? Now just maybe he is still trying to teach me that I need to rely upon his guidance. After all, his knowledge and timing are perfect in all things. I am sure he knows just who she is, for he knows when and what time he is going to bring her into my life. He knows my every need before I myself know it. I'm trying to keep this at the forefront of my knowledge as a believer in my God. But knowing that I'm living in the flesh and it being a very weak vessel, I find myself falling short of the glow of God as we all do at some point and time in our walk with him in this journey down this road we call life.

CROSSROADS OF LIFE

Now I do find myself at the crossroads in life, not knowing just which way I should go in this path that has been placed before me. For I do know that I must wait for my Heavenly Father to provide me with his road map that he has laid out for me to travel while in search of the most beautiful soul mate he has so created for me in the beginning and who has the other half of my soul, who is willing to take this journey with me down the hardest road that the two of us will travel in search of our true faith in our Heavenly Father as one. While as I sit here at the crossroads waiting for directions from my Heavenly Father about which way that I should go, I find myself reflecting on where he has brought me from on this journey in life. I can only say if I had kept my faith and trusted in him, not taking my eyes off him, I do believe that the first leg of my journey in life would not have ended up the way it did. Now I'm not saying that the journey was a bad one. But as for the second leg of my journey, I do believe it is going to be great, if not the best that one person could hope for in life. For he will bless me as he had Job. Satan did destroy everything that Job had worked for in his life. Even his wife, being the weaker vessel, fell to the temptation of the flesh and said to Job, "Why don't you just curse God and die?"

Job kept his faith in his God and was blessed even more so than before. Now I'm not saying I'm as great as Job was in God's eyes, but I do know and do believe in my Almighty God that he will always keep his word, for who-so-ever believes in him and accept him as their personal savior will have everlasting life in His kingdom.

Now I am sitting here at a place in my life, and I have not a clue on where I should go next in life. I find myself pondering what my fellow men think a single free man such as myself should do---that is to take the path down the ole rugged road that would lead me into the wilderness or to have an intimate relationship with any woman who is willing to have that kind of a relationship. To myself, that isn't the way that one should start a godly relationship. I myself believe that the relationship should be started out by the two of them putting God's will first in their life, and then all other things will play out as God planned it for them. Now I'm not suggesting that my fellow man isn't walking as close with their God as they may need to be. But just maybe need to check their soul with the way they are walking with their God. But who am I to say that their God doesn't said that it is very well and fine with him if the two partake in such a relationship? Who am I to say that one cannot fall to such a temp-ta-tion as to have an intimate relationship before marriage? I will leave this up to you to work out with your own salvation.

Now I find myself still here at the crossing of the roads. I ask myself, do I just turn around on this ole road in life that appears to be dusty and unclear, knowing that the dust will interfere with my sight staying focused on God? But I know that being in the flesh, my focus on my Lord God will become, for sure, cloudy, and therefore my sight will be interfered with. I know for a certainty from my past experience from traveling down an ole rugged dirt road that my thoughts will deceive me as to what may lay across the dusty dirt road ahead of me. I will not be able to know for certain if there is a bridge that may be crossing a river or if the bridge might be out. I must say there is so much uncertainty that lies before me. Will going back down this ole dirty and rugged road would be worth my time and effort, or even be in my best interest in doing so?

I know for certain that the most beautiful and mighty bridge that once had lay across the sparking clear blue river has once and for all been destroyed and cannot be rebuilt; it has been completely destroyed in the first journey of my relationship with someone I thought was my soul mate for all eternity, but somewhere at some point and time along the way the dust from this ole rugged dirt road became cloudy, and I somehow let it interfere with my journey in search of my true faith in my Almighty God, who I do believe created us to be together as one, to hold in the good time as well as the bad and for the riches and poor time as we continue our journey down an ole rugged road that God has placed before us. I must say right before the journey begins to end, I do not know just for certain if it was the dust from the ole dirt road or the smoke that came from the beautiful bridge being destroyed, but I do know from within my heart it was a journey that I can only thank my God for. It was the greatest and the most beautiful journey that one such as I could be on in their life, and it is one I will never forget as long as I shall live and travel in this journey we call life. I only hope and pray that as I do continue to travel in this life journey, I will not find myself making the same mistakes as before.

MISTAKES MADE

Now as the second leg of this journey of mine begins, I must say that there will be mistakes made. Life has taught me that no matter how hard you try in your life, you are going to make mistakes. After all, we do live in the flesh, and the flesh being a weak vessel, mistakes are going to be made. This is just some of what I do see from looking up into the rearview mirror and seeing nothing but a big cloud of dust coming from the ole rugged dirt road and a heavy dark smoke rising into the heaven from the mighty, beautiful bridge which once lay across the sparkling clear blue river that gently flows into the val-ley. Therefore, having seen this in my rearview mirror, I must tell you that turning around for me and going back down that ole rugged dirt road would not in any way be in my best interest; I must continue to look unto my God, who I do know has all the right answers to meet all my needs.

THE WEARY JOURNEY

I continue to travel this hard and weary journey in which I have found myself to be on in search of the most beautiful diamond in the rough whose rough edges God is still smoothing. I find myself continuing to ponder my weary inner thoughts on just which path that I should take that will be the best for me to please God and bring glory to him, for after all, did he not put us here to do just that, not to bring glory to our own self but to him and him alone, to be done as he has planned it? For you may ask, did he not give you your own free will to choose as you may? Yes, he gave to you the will to choose to do as you wish, but may I ask you one important thing? Do you think that it would not be in your best interest for you to accept his will for your life? For he did created you from the dust of the earth in his own image to serve him in all your faithfulness.

WILDEST DREAMS

But for I can only imagine in my wildest dreams on just how beautiful and amazing my helpmate will be whom my God has cer-tainly. She will be the most God-fearing soul mate that any man could ever hope for in his life. Just her love alone for God will bring the brightest sunshine when the darkest clouds covers the sun. In my darkest hours when my faith needs to be made stronger, she will lift me up to our God by her love alone. I likewise will do for her in her darkest hours of needs. For she is my beloved soulmate whom I will cherish for all eternity if we should live our lives under the canopy of heaven joined as one, being brought together by our faith by our Heavenly Father who we can believe in to supply our every need in our journey through life here on earth.

I can't help but to softly gaze into her beautiful eyes as they sparkle like the stars from the heaven's midnight sky. Her beautiful smile brings comfort to my soul, so does knowing she will always be there right by my side no matter how rough or hard things become in this journey of ours as we travel down this road we have found placed before us.

I sit here, and my thoughts on just where I should go from here are becoming very weary. Therefore, I must give my thoughts a little rest for a short time. How about we just take a coffee break? Are you okay with that? Hey, sounds good to me. After all, this is your story, and you are the one telling it.

A LOST SINNER

After giving my thoughts a rest, let's go back in time for a short insight on just what makes me who I am. Being born of the flesh and flesh being in sin, I was therefore born in sin, saying this sin itself will destroy the entire inner being of the person you are to be in life. I came to know Jesus at a young age in my life, but not knowing him for who he is or what he would come to mean to me later in life. Now I began the journey through life as a sinner without salvation, being doomed for eternity to live in the torment of the endless lake of fire. I came to realize that I was just a lost sinner without salvation, and I learned that Jesus came into this world to give us all a new chance in life, those who would accept him as their personal savior. By our own sins being placed upon him, he suffered much agony so that we could be born again of the spirit and have our rightful place in our Father's mansion, which is in heaven.

I find myself asking a question, just how did sin come about in this world? Satan brought so much confusion into our Father's kingdom by trying to take over God's throne. By him trying this, God kicked him and a third of his angels out of heaven. Satan, knowing that man and woman was made from the dust of the earth, knew it would be easier to take over the flesh than it would be the spirit; he could deny us our rightful place in the kingdom of our Father. Therefore, Jesus's blood had to become the atonement for the sins of this world, for us to be able to reclaim our rightful place in God's kingdom. But before this could take place, Jesus first had to be born by miraculous spiritual birth, being born of a virgin woman who has not been known by a man, for if the virgin woman had been touched by a man of the flesh, then the blood of Jesus would have become tarnished with sin; the man, being of the flesh himself, is born in sin. Therefore, Jesus's birth could only be of a virgin woman. For the virgin part of woman had not became tarnished by sin by knowing a man. Jesus was born into this world to teach the truthful way of our Father.

THE TRUE WAY

Now Jesus himself made his journey through this old sinful world, teaching the true way in which we should live out our lives as to please our Heavenly Father. He himself faced the same trials and tribulations as we all do in life and much more, such as having been spit upon, having his beard plucked, being beaten half to death, then ultimately, having a crown of thorns placed upon his head and being laughed at. Moreover, he was then nailed to an old rugged cross, his side pierced with a spear. He was sacrificed for us all to have our rightful place in the most beautiful mansion in the kingdom of our God Almighty. Amen. Jesus had taken all our sins upon himself, for he knew that we were born of the flesh and could not withstand Satan's powerful temptation of our flesh. Now this being said, my dear beloved brother and sisters, may I ask, do you think for one minute that you have faced more suffering in your life than Jesus? Well, if you do, you may need to check your faith and who you put your trust in. I'm not saying that you have not been saved or anything, but you may need to spend more time in your prayer closet than worrying about something you don't have any control over. If you intend on making the kingdom of God your eternal home, you must first accept the truth that you yourself are a lost sinner in who needs Jesus's blood to wash away your selfish uncontrollable sins. You must confess with your mouth that you are a lost sinner in order to receive a room in mansion that no man can build with his hands alone under the canopy of heaven.

DEEPEST THOUGHTS

As I sit here in my deepest thoughts on which way this journey may take me, I find myself looking down the road that goes into the valley where so many beautiful flowers are beginning to flourish by a crystal clear blue stream giving its much-needed nutrients to them, so they grow so much more beautiful and brighter than the day my God has blessed me with. I start this journey on a road that leads into the valley. I begin to wonder, could it be that my most beloved soul mate may be among these beautiful wildflowers growing by this stream of the living water, becoming so much more beautiful than anything known to man under the canopy of heaven?

SPARKLING STREAMS

As I stand here by the sparkling streams, I feel a gentle cool breeze come across my face. I gaze out across the beautiful valley of wild-fowlers, and I couldn't help but notice a very beautiful flower leaning slightly over into the clear stream as if to take a sip of its living water. As I see this beautiful flower slightly leaning into the crystal clear stream, I'm reminded of a woman who knelt at the old rugged cross where our beloved Jesus hung that day. Upon that cross where he hung, a Roman soldier was ordered to pierced his side, and from his side there came a flow of blood and water that gently flowed down the hill into the stream that runs through the valley, providing ever-lasting living water. Whosoever is willing to partake of it will have everlasting life.

May I ask, are you willing to take a drink from this stream of life? Knowing that your life would be forever changed. For I stand here once again at the crossroads, pondering my most inner thoughts. As I looked straight before me, I see what appears to a steep hill that leads into the beautiful sky above me. Now I let my imagination run free as to what could be along the pathway of the journey going up that hill.

THE GREAT HILL

I begin to question myself, am I truly prepared to start such a great journey up such a great hill as this one? Knowing that there could possibly be mudslides caused by the heavy rains and some fall-ing rocks as well. Knowing these things, I find myself thinking, could it be possible that the most beautiful soul mate God has ever created for me is somewhere along the way up this great hill that is before me?

I try to figure out how to best prepare myself for such a great journey; this appears to be one of the most challenging I have ever faced in my entire life. But just knowing in my heart that the most beautiful, God-fearing soul mate could be somewhere along that long difficult journey up that hill can make it become the easiest one that I could ever face in life. But knowing all this, I still find myself asking, are you willing to sacrifice everything you have ever worked for in your life, to just let it go and follow that old road up a great hill in search of a soul mate that you think you are in so much need of? I must ask one thing of you, could it be that the soul mate you think you need just might be the spirit of the Lord? With this question being asked of me, I take my own advice and go into my own prayer closet. I need to do some deep soul-searching before I can even consider taking on such a great challenge at this point and time in my life.

In my own prayer closet, I begin to search deep within myself, asking my Father for knowledge and wisdom and understanding, as well as the know-how to reach out to someone who has not yet come to know and accept our Lord Jesus as their personal savior. They have no way of understanding just what it means to have someone that you are able to lay all your burdens upon. For Jesus said, "Come unto me, all ye that labor and are heavy laden, and I will give you rest." With this in mind, we know as believers in Christ that no matter what kind of situation we may find ourselves in, we can turn it over to our Lord Jesus Christ.

I must say unto you, my friend, that you will not get the answer if it is not in the will of God that you receive you answer on whatever it is that you have asked of him. I tell you that you, first and foremost, must be born again of the spirit before God can ever begin working in your life. Now let's take a look at 1 Thessalonians Chapter 5: Verse 18–19, "I find that it says, rejoice evermore, pray without ceasing. For in everything give thanks, for this is the will of God in Christ Jesus concerning you. Quench not the spirit."

For I say unto you all, let the spirit of life from our Lord breathe life into their nostrils. Our Lord God's spirit, being free within you, can and will guide you if you will open your ears to you heart and hear him, but first you need to accept the fact that he is the creator of life before he can begin his work in your life in a way that you will find peace and happiness in every situation that you find yourself in. There is much to be thankful for. God did give you the free choice to serve him as your personal savior and have a place with him for eternity in his mansion. I found myself here once again, thinking that I'm alone, but in reality, I am not alone. After all, didn't our Lord say he would not leave us or forsake us? How can I be all alone in my search for the most beautiful soul mate God has created from my rib, as he did for Adam in the beginning?

CHOOSING A PATH

As I begin this journey, I believe my God knows just when and where I will meet her. For I see now there are so many different paths that is layer before me., for I must now choose the right path which is more suitable for me to travel. I see there are so many dif-ferent types of wildflowers receiving their needed nutrients from the stream that is running through the valley. For I can see by the way they are growing from receiving their nutrients; they are living their life by the words and faith of our God. For some reason, I have not yet found the one wildflower that appeals to my need. I find myself asking, could it be that just because they're receiving the nutrients from the living water, they are letting the weeds and thorns choke out their beauty?

THE LONELY VALLEY

I shall continue the search through this beautiful but lonely valley looking for the one only wildflower who is drinking from the living stream of water that provides eternal life with our living God. Now I begin to ponder on just how one would be able to recognize her beauty among all the other wildflowers who are also drinking from the pure living water of life. Who am I to seek for such a beau-tiful and pure woman as this to be with a wretch such as me? I find within myself not knowing of the right answer. As it stands right now, the only answer I can give you is for me to spend more time in my own pray closet, seeking the will of our living God, knowing in due time, he will reveal unto me the right answer, which I will need to search for my beloved helpmate.

As I now begin my stroll through the living words, down by the sparking crystal clear river I find in these words of "Lemuel," "for who can find a virtuous woman? For her price is for above rubies. For the heart of her husband doth safely trust in her, so that he shall have no need to spoil. For she will do him good and not bring evil to him for all the days of her life. For she seethe wool, and flax and worth willingly with her hands to bring honor to her beloved husband, and for her husband will be willingly to work hard with his hands right beside her, all the days, for I say unto you in these days and time in which we are now living in, for it must take both doing their part in lifting each other up in the good time as well in the bad times, for Satan is on the loose and is seeking and trying to destroy every marriage that our God has let be put together by our own free will. For all marriage are not approved by God." (Proverbs Chapter 31 verse 10-13)

Now with this being said, let's go back to the living words of "Lemuel"

> *"Give not they strength unto women, nor thy ways to that which destroyed kings. For it is not for men to drink wine; nor for princess strong drink. Lest they drink, and forget the law and pervert the judgment of any of the afflicted. Give strong drink unto him that is perish, and wine unto those that be of heavy hearts. Let him drink and forget his poverty and remember his misery no more. Open thy mouth for the dumb in cause of all such as are appointed to destruction. Open thy mouth, judge righteously, and plead the cause of the poor and needy, placing their needs before they own needs, for I say unto you, if you are willing to place the needs of others before your own needs and you do it with the right intentions of pleasing our heavenly father, he will surely bless you more so then you have ignored the needs of others." (Proverbs 31:3-16)*

Now the search must continue. I must move forward in the living word if I am to find my answer. I find my heart feeling heavy from searching for an answer where there may be no answer. I find myself asking from within myself, could it be that Satan is trying to deceive me and keep me from searching out what is rightly mine, which was given to me by my Heavenly Father from the beginning of time? I must find within myself the strength of my spirit to put on the whole armor of our living God to fight this battle that I now find myself, for it appears as if I am being attacked from all sides. I must go to the living words of Ephesians to find the inspiration I need to put on the whole armor of God:

> *"For it is a shame even to speak of those things which are done of them in secret, but all things that are reproved*

are made manifest by the light for whatsoever doth make manifest is light. Wherefore he saithe awake thou that sleepiest and arise from the dead, and Christ shall give thee light. See then that ye elk circumspectly, not as fools, but as wise, redeeming the time, because the day are evil. Wherefore be ye not unwise but understanding of what the will of our lord is for you in these evil times. I say unto you, be not drunk with wine, wherein is excess; for I say be filled with the spirit by the spirit of our lord God. Speaking unto yourselves in psalms and hymns and spiritual songs, singing and making melody in your heart unto our Lord." Ephesians Chapter 5 verse (12-17)

Now my search takes me on a journey deeper into the words of Ephesians, where I find giving thanks always for all things unto God and the father in the name of our Lord Jesus Christ. I do believe if we would just take the time out and give thanks unto our Lord, we would find the peace and joy our hearts need to forgive one another, ever as God for Christ's sake has forgiven you your sins. I therefore say unto you all, be followers of our Lord God as dear children, my brothers and sisters, my prayers being that you come to know Christ as your personal savior. Amen.

WEEK OF EASTER

The week of Easter is the time in which we as believers in Christ recall the resurrection of our Lord Jesus Christ. I ask, are we not called to share the true gospel of our living God, who lives within us? I know this to be true in my heart as a believer of faith, and my faith being in Christ. May I ask this of you, in what way are you sharing the true gospel of our living Jesus Christ? I know all things works to the good of those who choose to serve the Lord. Are you serving in a way to bring glory to God the highest, or are you serving in a way to bring glory unto you? I feel that if this is what you are doing, then I must tell you that your glory is going to bring unto you a big disappointment to you in the end. But the glory in which you bring before the most high will last you for all eternity.

I find in Matthew 23:25 Jesus speaking to the people about cleaning the outside of the cup and of the platter, but within they are full of extortion and excess. I see that he is referring to the cup as being the body of the flesh, full of self-righteousness. Therefore, we must first clean the inside of the body, being the spirit, which is full of our own self-righteousness. I feel with in my own heart that our self-righ-teousness will get us nowhere but a place that is an eternal lake of fire and torment. Ye serpent, ye generation of vipers, how can we escape the damnation of hell? Only by the confession of your mouth that you are a lost sinner without salvation and then accept-ing the fact that Jesus did shed his own blood on the old rugged cross for your sins.

"Now, O Jerusalem, Jerusalem, thou have kill the prophets, and stones them which are sent unto thee, how often would I have gathered you together as my own, as a mother hen gathered her chickens under wings, and you would not come unto me. For I say unto you, you shall not see me hence fore, till ye shall say blessed is he that cometh in the name of the lord" (Matthew 23:37–39).

THE WELL OF LIFE

say unto you all no matter what kind of situation you may be facing in your life, there is only one true friend; that friend is Jesus Christ. Jesus is the only friend you can rely on to see you through the hard times in life. There's a well that is deeper than my most inner thoughts. The well I'm referring to is the well of blood of our Lord Jesus Christ. For his blood, there is no well that can contain it, and no dam that can hold it or slow the flow of his blood, which he gave up so freely for undeserving wrecks like me. There is no way in my deepest thoughts that I can't even begin to imagine under the canopy of heaven just what he must have seen in me, for him to lay down his own life. There is only one thing that I can say, could it just be that what he saw was what our Father had created was so beautiful, he didn't want to see it destroyed by Satan and his angels?

The minute speck of Jesus's blood possessed so much power that there's no way a human mind can ever begin to understand it. His blood can heal a person. Just touching the hem of his garment, the woman with the issue of blood was healed. Now that is power. The book of Luke, chapter 4, verse 33 speaks of such great power. Now look back to verses 18–19:

> *"The spirit of the lord is upon me, because he baptized and anointed me to preach the gospel to the poor; he also sent me to heal the broken hearted, to preach deliverance to the captives, and recovering of sight to the blind, to set*

at liberty them that are bruised, to preach the acceptable year of the lord. For the power of his blood hoes true also in these days in which we are living in."

I say unto you, if you do not believe his words holds true, just look at your reflection in a mirror and say that there is no living God. Your reflection in that mirror is a true sign of a living God, who gave his own begotten son Jesus. Whosoever believes in him, their sins will be forgiven, and they will have the everlasting life with him in his mansion.

I find myself asking this question, just why it is so hard for some people to accept the fact that there is a living God? I guess one could say, there are people like the days before Jesus came into this world to be the last final sacrifice for all mankind. I have heard some people say that God would not allow evil things come upon his people. How about we just take a good look in the book of Job so we may see what evil came upon him.

In chapter 42, verse 11, they bemoaned him and comforted him over all the evil that the Lord had brought upon him. Job was considered to be just one of the most perfect and upright and one that feared God and eschewed evil, for there came a day when the sons of God came unto him to present themselves before the Lord, and there came Satan also among them. The Lord said unto Satan, "Whence comets thou?"

Satan answered the Lord and said, "From going to and from the earth and walking up and down in it."

God asked Satan if he has considered his servant Job.

With is in mind, could it be when you find yourself facing what you see to be a hard time in life, it just may be that Satan has come before God once again. God has asked Satan if he has considered you as he did his servant Job. For God knows who his true servant are and just how they will respond to everything that Satan can and will bring upon them.

Jesus said, "If you have as much faith as a seed of mustard, you can move mountains."

TRUE FAITH

Just where can you find such faith? Only in Jesus's powerful blood, which he gave up so freely that day. We as sinners crucified him upon that cross. Chapter 2, verse 3, the Lord asks Satan once again if he considered his servant Job, that there is none like him in the earth—a perfect an upright man, one that feared God and eschewed evil?

> "And still he heath fast his integrity, although thou movers me against him, to destroy him without cause. Satan answered the lord and said, skin for skin, yea all that man that will give for his life. But forth thine hand now, and touch his bone and his flesh, and he will curse thee to thy face. And the Lord said to Satan, behold he is in thine hand; but save his life. For satan smote Job with sore boils from the sole of his feet unto his crown of his head. Job took potsherd to scrape himself withal; and sat down among the ashes. Then his wife said unto him, dost thou still retain thine integrity? Why don't you just curse God and die. For Job said unto her, thou speak as one of the foolish women spiked. What? Shall we receive good at the hand of God, and shall we not receive evil? In all of this did not Job sin with his lips." Job Chapter 2 verse (3-10)

Jesus himself has not at this time gave up his blood as a sacrifice for mankind. All Job had were the words of the prophets who came before him. He was still able to keep his integrity and sin not. For it appears that there are people living in this world nowadays who have no clue of knowing just what it means to have integrity. Just what dose integrity mean to you? Well, this is a question only you can answer from within your own self.

Now as for myself the true meaning of integrity, simply it is the quality of being honest and having strict moral principles, moral uprightness, and the state of whole and undivided upholding terri-to-rial integrity and national sovereignty, for I say by me holding on to this true meaning of integrity, my every need will be met in life, and the wants will take care of themselves in the end. Not to see myself being as a great man such as Job. For Job held fast to his integrity and sinned not, and God so blessed him with more than he had before Satan came against him. Satan came upon him, trying to get him to curse God to his face. Satan was trying to show God that there is no perfect person under the canopy of heaven, but in the end, God showed him. For that are some people he created that will hold fast to their integrity unto end of time. I must keep my integrity in check and intact if I'm going to make the kingdom of God, my home. Amen.

THE AROMA OF SPRING

For spring is now in the air. I can feel the a slightly warm breeze blowing across the valley where so many wildflowers are growing so beautifully and in so many different shapes and sizes and colors; they spring up by the crystal clear blue stream of the living water. One can only imagine just which one of those beautiful wildflowers will con-tinue to keep their true integrity of her faith, which she has received by drinking from the stream of the living water, which she has been drinking from since the first day she was planted in the lonely valley of life.

For the seasons of this lonely life here in the valley will continue to change as each day brings forth different events in our lives. There appears to be many different kind wildflowers growing in this valley of life. I must keep a close watch on my heart to not to get caught up in the deception of the false integrity of the different kind of wildflower. For beauty lies within the soul of that beautiful young flower who is growing up freely and so innocently by drinking from the crystal stream of the living water of life flowing freeing from our Heavenly Father. I must once again return unto the living word to find the true answer on such a great matter, on how to distinguish the difference in choosing the right kind of wildflower that is growing so beautifully out by the living stream of water.

Now looking in the book of "Ezra," Chapter 10 verse 2-3, Elam answered and said unto Ezra, "For we have trespassed against our God, and have taken strange wives of the people of the land: yet now there is hope in Israel concerning this thing. Now therefore let us make a covenant with our God to put away all the wives, and such is born of them, according to the counsel of my Lord, and of those that tremble at the commandment of our God, and let it be done according to the law. For they gave their word, that they would put away their strange wives; and being guilty they offered up a ram from their flock, for their trespass against God."

TRUE INTEGRITY

For it would be in your best interest to know the true integrity of the beautiful flower that you plan on take from the valley. There have been a lot of great men broken down by many of those beautiful flowers, of whom integrity was not well rooted by the living water as needed to be.

Taking a look at 2 Samuel 11.

> "David arose from off his bed and walked upon the roof of the king's house; and from the roof he saw a woman washing herself and the woman was very beautiful to look upon. David being the man he was, seat and inquired after the woman. For one said, is this not Bath-Sheba the wife of Uriah? David then sent a messengers, and took her and she came unto him, and he lay with her, for she was purified from her uncleanness; and she then returned unto her house and the woman conceived and sent and told David that she was with child. David ask for Uriah to come unto him for David was trying to get him to lay with his wife. But Uriah being a man of true integrity would not go unto his own house to lay with his wife."

David knew in his own heart that he had failed his own integrity and committed a sin before his God. I now look unto the book of Genesis for more answers as to what one may need to watch out for in choosing a good soul mate. Chapter 18, verse 11, says "Now

Abraham and his wife Sarah were old and well stricken in age; and he said, I will certainly return unto thee according to time of life; and so, Sarah thy wife shall have a son, for Sarah heard this from the tent door, which was behind him. There Sarah laughed within herself saying after I am waxed old shall I have pleasure, my lord being old also. For the lord ask Abraham wherefore did Sarah laugh, saying shall I surety bear a child which am old? And Sarah denied saying I laughed not, for she was afraid. And he said way; but thoug didst laugh."

For Abraham also failed in his integrity, as did Sarah; by laughing at what was told Abraham. Abraham let her persuade him into laying with his bondwoman and bore a child, by her. Look what took place with Lot and his two daughters.

Now look into Judges 13–16. It portrays Samson as a man who was given great strength by God, but who ultimately lost his strength by letting his integrity down by telling Delilah just wherein his strength was. Delilah told the Philistines to shave his hair off his slumber (Judges 16–19). Samson was born into an Israelite family the son of Mariah.

For my journey through the prophets of old time, Isaac was deceived by his beloved wife, Rebekah, who deceived him into giving Jacob his brother Esau's blessing. Now I see the deception of what was to be true integrity and there was none as it appears.

I continue in my journey down this old rugged dirt road I am traveling on, not knowing just what may be lying across the road ahead of me. Now looking back at these great men of god, Job, for now, is the only one who kept his true integrity with God. I pray that my God from upon the high will guide my every step that I will take as I begin my search for that beautiful soul mate, knowing she will be the most god-fearing woman that a man such as I could ever dream of having in one's life. For is it better to have once loved and lost that true love than not to have ever known what it really means to have had a true love in your life at least once.

I look out across the wide-open plain just admiring the beau-ti-ful wildflowers as the warm summer breeze from off the steam so gently blows the young and so innocent wildflowers from one side to the other, as if they are waving their beautiful silky soft petals unto the heavens above, from where the warm breeze comes from.

THE STREAM OF LIFE

As I move ever so slowly over this open plain admiring these lovely wildflowers, I come up on a stream, and I see across the way what appears to be a woman dipping her water pail in to the stream, for her to carry back home for her family to drink and prepare their supper. The stream is so wide at this point that I'm not able to get across to assist her with her pails of water, so I begin to journey up and down this stream in search of a narrow place to cross to assist her on her journey in carrying the water home to her family. Even though I find there are so many beautiful wildflowers on this side of the stream, there appears to be more flowers coming and going on the other side of the stream in search of the living water, which provides the much-needed nutrition for life to be sustained on this planet where we are live. Could it be that my true beloved soul mate just might be on the other side of this stream that flows from the most high?

MEADOWS OF LIFE

As I leave the open plain of life and walk ever so slowly through the meadow of life. I find myself once again surrounded by the love-liest wildflowers one could find himself to be around. As I continue to walk, I hear coming through the soft warm summer breeze what appears to be the voice of an angel singing a beautiful song, "Begin for he will see you through the fire once again." As I continue to listen to the song, I come up on a bed of red clovers, and the voice appears to get a little closer. I then take a seat in the bed of clovers. I continue to listen to the song of the angel singing her praise unto our Lord. I looked and there appeared to be an angel sitting beside me, and I reach out to caress her beautiful soft cheeks. She began to speak ever so slowly as my fingers begin to move across her rosy red lips. I look into her eyes, which appears to be blue as the heaven's sky, and as I look closer into her eyes, I see them sparkling like the stars of heaven's midnight skies. My finger slowly moves softly across her cheek to her silky long autumn hair, and I softly stroke my fingers though her long soft hair.

She placed one of her hands upon my chest, and my heart began to flutter as she spoke these words into my ears, "For our time has not yet come, for I know not if we can ever be together as one under the canopy of heaven."

These words that she spoken into my ears brought forth tears into my eyes, and they flowed down my cheeks as if the heavenly skies had released her rain upon me. She continues to speak with that soft angel voice. She says to hold on for just a little longer, for our time will surely come in due time, in God's will.

My heart began to beat once again, knowing that there is still hope in this life of mine. Now I find myself facedown before my Heavenly Father asking for his mercy to be upon me. I must arise and continue my lonely journey unto the blue crystal clear stream that flows for eternity to renew my heartbroken spirit that lives within its sinful flesh that came from the dust of the earth if I'm to continue such a great journey in search of a beautiful helpmate. I know somewhere out there, I will find that powerful stream of living water to renew my broken heart.

A HEARD JOURNEY

So I found myself to be out of the meadow where the wild-flow-ers were growing ever so beautifully. Now I am traveling into the open desert, where there appears to be nothing but scorching sand. For the sun is shining upon this old flesh of me. Now the heat has been beaming down on me now for the past four days. Being without water and food, I find myself becoming weaker. I began to wonder if I can keep myself going to find a place to stay for a short time to rest my weary mind and maybe find water to quench the dying soul-scorching thirst that appears to be bringing me to my knees. I find myself trusting my Lord, asking him to show me the way in which I should go to find such a place, wherein I may find water and food to strengthen my body and thoughts.

As I continue my journey in search of the most beautiful soul mate who is drinking from the living stream of life, I have become very weak and passed out from exhaustion that has been placed upon me by the heat of this desert. I have now awakened to find myself in the presence of what appears to be some beautiful angels. They were standing over me with their palm branches cooling me while one was trying to give me a cool drink of her living water, which came from the stream of life. I looked and beheld one with food for my weak body. All at once, I truly awakened from what some would say to be just a hallucination from the scorching heat of this desert. As I do rise from the scorching heat, I begin to ponder weakly on just which way I should go in this deserted desert place I have found myself to be in. I must stay on my true course to find an answer on this matter. Where I'm to find such a beautiful soul mate who is truly drinking from the crystal clear blue stream of life. For I must surely find the living water somewhere a long this journey of me in this desert. I now find myself to be coming upon what appear to be a beautiful wildflower, only to realize it to be just a desert cactus full of thorns growing in this oasis.

As I attempt to restrict water from the cactus to quench the scorching dying thirst that is within my throat, I look up and I see in the far distance what appears to be a caravan headed in my direction. I cannot call out unto them because my throat has been parched by the desert heart. I must in some way figure out a way to bring forth the living water from this cactus, which will hopefully quench my thirst. For I need to be able to call out unto that caravan that is moving in my direction if I going to make it out of this desert alive. I take my knife from off my side and stab the cactus, cutting a small hole into the center of it, and out flows the living water that would surely quench my dying thirst.

I would like to have a cup of coffee right about now, I'm thinking I may have some in mine bag. Now my thirst has been quince by the water that is now flowing from the cactus. As I see the caravan moves ever so slowly toward me, I begin to hear their voices being carried by the soft warm breeze that is blowing ever so gently across this desert. I must save the little strength that is within me for a little longer until the caravan draws a little closer before I call out unto them for their help in rescuing me from this hot scorching heat that I now find myself to be in. I can now see what appears to be the most gorgeous caravan of wildflowers that any man has ever laid his eyes upon within his lifetime. Now the caravan has gotten closer, I begin to cry out with a loud voice as they moved closer toward me. For one of the wildflower spoke with a soft angelical voice asking, "Why is a man like yourself doing way out here alone?"

"I will answer your question, but before I do, may I ask of you for a cool drink of your water to quench my thirst."

She answers, "Sir, you may have a drink of my water to quench your dying thirsty."

I took from her the living water and begin drink of it, and as I did so, I could feel my life begin to come back within me. It was then that I begin to tell her my story.

As I begin to tell her my story as to why I came to be in this deserted place, she stopped me and asked me, "Sir, would you like to join our caravan on our journey unto our father's mansion?" I answered her, "Yes, I would love to go with you on your journey to you father's home." I climbed upon the back of the camel with her. The camel begin to rise to its feet and walk in the same direction which appeared to me as the same direction in which they came from.

I asked a dumb question, "Why does it appear that we are head in the same direction in which you came from?" She smiled the most beautiful smile that I have ever been in the presence of. She begins to speak with that angelic voice of her. She said, "You have been out here way too long in this scorching desert heat, and your mind is now beginning to play tricks on you, for I can ensure you, we are not traveling in the same direction in which we have come."

As she continued to speak, "For in two days travel we will be at our father's mansion, and there I can nurse you back to somewhat of good health."

By now my eyes had begun to grow heavy with sleep, and I find myself laying my head upon the back of her soft warm shoulder, my face covered with her silky long hair as to block the hot sun from beaming down on my face.

She must have just washed her hair, for her hair has the scent of coconut milk. While in my deepest sleep, I begin to dream a dream that I cannot begin to describe, for it was unlike any dream that I have had ever before. I awakened from my sleep to find myself to be surrounded by the most gorgeous group of flowers placed around me, as if I had died in my sleep. As I begin to stand, she placed one of the most gorgeous flowers upon my chest and began to speak with her sweet soft angelic voice unto me, "You need to rest for a little while longer."

I responded with a soft smile of my only and said, "for you don't understand, I must arise and be on my way."

She said, "Sir, you are the one that don't understand, you are in no shape to travel on in this desert."

Well, I guess for now I can be here for just a little while longer, at least until I can catch the next caravan moving out.

For two weeks now, I have been in this dried-up desert in search of the living water that is bringing forth the much-needed nutrient that is feeding these gorgeous flowers that I have now found myself to be surrounded by. I know for sure that the crystal clear blue stream is flowing somewhere very close by here. If it did not, then these beautiful flowers surely could not continue to survive in this desert. I continue to observe the moments of these gorgeous flowers carrying out their daily duties. I see one carrying what appears to be a water pail headed to the courtyard of thy father's mansion. As I move in a little closer to get a better look to see just what it was that she was caring, she looks up and saw that I was watching her. She begin to smile and motion unto me, as to say come on follow her, so I begin to follow her, we came up to a well, and we begin to talk about the well of water. As we continue to talk, I find myself reaching out to assist her in drawing the water from well. As I do, my hands meet hers. As our hands touch, she slowly pulls hers back. I look in to her eyes and ask, "Did I do something wrong?"

She once again smiled her lovely smile and said in that soft voice of hers, "No, you did not do anything wrong."

I asked, "Why did you pull back your hand from me?" She answers by saying, "For you do not understand." "Understand what, may I ask?"

She begins to tell that she has a much heavier burden placed upon her than anybody knows about. I find myself not knowing just what to say next in a situation such as this one. I do find her to be one of the most attractive wildflowers that I have ever met so far in this journey while traveling down this old rugged dusty road here in the desert. I have asked myself time after time, just what do I do now? Do I come right out and just ask her just what it could be that has got her so burdened down? That would cause her to pull away when I try to get to know just what it is that makes her who she is.

ONES INNER THOUGHTS

Oh, for so many times now, I have found myself pondering my deepest inner thoughts, and now once again, I ask myself just what do one do in a situation such as this one. Should I continue to try talking with this beautiful and attractive wildflower or not, knowing that there could possibly be many more beautiful women out there in is this old world who are also alone and in search of someone to share in their journey of life with.

As I sit here on the steps of thy father's mansion enjoying the warm summer breeze, for I catch a glimpse from out of the corner of my eye of someone approaching me from the side of the stamps, I look around and there appear the most beautiful breathtaking woman I have ever lay eye upon. Whom I follow the day before to the well to draw water with.

She asks, "How are you today??"

SIMPLY BREATHTAKING

Her beauty has taken my breath away, and all I could say unto her is that I was doing okay. I guess one could say, from within my heart and soul, there is so much more I would love to say unto her, but not knowing just how she may feel toward me, I must keep my most desirable feelings locked away with in my soul.

She asked, "May I sit here beside you for little while to rest my feet and catch my breath?"

I responded with a yes, "I would love to have your company." As she sit down on the steps beside me, we begin to talk, and I tell her about the journey in which I am on in search of a the most god-fearing woman who has put him first in her life and is so will-ing to put the needs of her family first and foremost, and how it has become much harder to find in this time we are living in now.

She asks, "Is this how you came to be out here in this desert all alone?"

I answered her with a yes. She begins to smile and say, "Wish you the best of luck on finding such a woman out here in this desert."

I turned unto her and said, "Well, thank you, I think. I must continue my journey out in this hot scorching desert and go unto a place more suitable for such a woman."

She asks, "Just where would you go to find such a place, and would you be so willing to take me when you go?"

These words she has spoken into my ears, "Would you be so willing to take me with you when you go?"

LOVELY BROWN EYES

I turned unto her and looked very softly into those lovely brown eyes of hers, and my heart begin to once again to flutter, as if it was going to stop beating. I became unable to respond unto her request. She reached out and took my hand into hers, and I begin to caress hers. It was at that time I was able to catch my breath and get my heart back in tune. Then I was able to answer her, "Yes, but I must ask you, are you sure that this is what you truly want to do? Leave everything that you have here and go with me on such a great journey even if I know not where I am going or how long I will be gone on this journey of mine in search of such a lovely woman?"

She responded with, "I have nothing here but a very heavy burden of my own."

It was at that point in time that I just wanted to say unto her is, "I would love for you to place your heavy burdens upon my chest and your troubles in my pocket and rest your love upon me for a little while."

We continued to sit out there together and enjoy each other's company on the steps of thy father's house. I find within myself asking this question, "How can you think for one minute that a woman with such beauty in which you cannot even describe, think that she would be willing to do that for she knows very little about me?"

She began to tell me, "A caravan is to be going out tomorrow in search for some livestock that has gone astray." She asked me, "Would you like to join up with the caravan and see if I could in anyway find my way out of this dessert?"

I answered her with a "Yes! I would love to do just that."

She asked, "Are you still planning to take me with you?"

I had to ask her one more time "Are you sure that's what you want to do?"

Before I could give her my answer on such a great matter as this, I tried my best to explain to her once we get started, there is no turning back from this journey that I am on.

She replied unto me, saying, "I have never ever been surer of anything in my life than this."

So, my replyed unto this beautiful wildflower was "yes." I would love to have you with me on this journey.

A ROMANTIC NIGHT

So we left and went our separate ways. As I was having supper that night, she came in all dressed up in a beautiful red sun dress, with her silky long hair draped across both shoulders, revealing her smooth silky skin and a smile on her face that could light up a dark room when she walked in. I could not help but watch her as she sashayed across the room headed in my direction.

I reached out for my glass of sweet tea to take a drink. As I did, she appeared before me and asked, "May I join you for supper?"

I replied with, "Yes, you may."

I stood up and pull out her chair so she could be seated at the table with me. I asked the waitress to come over and take her order. She ordered a glass of sweet tea to drink and to eat lamb chop, mashed taters and gravy, and a dinner roll. As we begin to eat our dinner, we talked about just how long we thought it would take us to find our way out of desert. Little did I know, she was also looking for her a soul mate to spend her life with.

My Lord, I'm asking of you to help me in finding the right way to express the feeling that I have for her, for they are hidden way down deep within my soul, and I know not how to get them to come forward. For she is one of the most caring persons you have put before me since I have been on this lonely journey of me. Maybe I am going about this in the wrong way. Should I just come straight out and ask her just what it is that she's searching for in a relationship with a man that could possibly be her soul mate? How can I expect her to express her feeling when I myself am afraid to express my true feeling about her? For could it be that she is just overwhelmed with the burdens that have been placed upon her. That she not should of what she is looking for in a relationship with a man. For she has been done wrong for so many time in her life and is now scared on taking a chance with someone who is wanting to love her for who she is. Finishing our dinner, I asked her what time was the caravan to be leaving out tomorrow.

She answered, "Sometime between eight to ten o'clock."

We say good night, and we went to our own rooms. I got ready for bed, but for the life of me, I could not fall asleep. I was thinking about how great it is going to be to leave this hot scorching desert. I don't know just what time I did fall asleep. I do not recall anything until I heard a knock at the door asking, "Are you up?" It is time to go meet the caravan. I jump up and got dressed and grabbed my bags and ran out the door as if I had been shot out of a cannon, not wanting to miss the caravan leaving. I am one person wanting to get out of this desert and go to a place where I am more accustomed to.

HORRIFYING SANDSTORMS

We get about a half day's journey out from thy father's man-sion, and I look out across the horizon. I see what appears to be headed in our direction one of the most horrifying sandstorms one has ever seen in their lifetime of living in this desert. I find myself asking just what one does in this situation. For after all, we do not have a storm pit out here in the desert.

Okay, for after all, we are in a desert. Someone suggested that we need to put the caravan of camels all together in one big circle and have them to lay down. We tie one to another and then tied ourselves one to the other and then ties ourselves to the camels. By the time we got all this done, the sandstorm was upon us. I, for one, begin to pray that we all would not die out here in this desert. The sand-storm was beginning to pile up all around us, as if we are going to be buried alive. It was at that point in time in my life. I reach out to her, pulling her closer into my arms. I was going to tell her the truth about the way I was beginning to feel about her. But the sandstorm was over. The camels began to stand up, picking us up with them, for we were tied to their side just for that reason, to be able to find one another, and it worked. For we all survived the most horrifying sandstorm that anyone we know of has ever been in. So we got back on the camels and started our journey once again. We are now day and a half out on this journey.

I can feel that it will not be much longer before we get to a place in which I can say farewell to some of the most lovely and beautiful wildflowers that one could find growing in the desert. In a way, I was kind feeling sad about having to leave them out here in this desert alone now that I know just what is like to be in a desert all alone. Oh heck, they don't need someone like me for they know how to survive; they just came through one of the most horrifying sandstorms that anyone has ever been in. What was I just thinking? I just want to get out of this place. It seems like a lifetime that I have been out here in this desert. It has been now going on nine weeks, too long for someone like me to be out here in this desert. But I can say this for sure, this is not been my first time that I have been in a desert. I have visited the deserts of the Middle East on a short vacation in the early nineties. This has no reflection on the journey I am now going through as far as being in the desert.

ONE NIGHT IN THE DESERT

Now the caravan that I have been with has been on the move for three whole days. As the third day is coming to its end, we stop and begin to pitch our tents for the night. I become hungry and go out looking for some wood to build a fire with in order to prepare a meal for myself to eat. I arrive back to where I have my tent set up with some wood for the fire. I find myself with having company. Once again there she stood, the most amazing woman my eyes ever beheld. She was wearing a peach-colored blouse, with her black silky hair draped across one shoulder, and she had the smile of an angel. When I see her smile, it makes my heart beat with joy knowing that such a beautiful woman has a smile such as hers. It can bring a lovely warm feeling to my heart. I haven't felt this wonderful in quite some time within myself. As I begin to get the fire going to cook our food, I find my hunger being replaced by the desire of just being in her presence. When I am in her presence, I find myself saying and doing things I would not normally say or do. She must have cast spell upon me. Now I can't see nothing more than her beauty, oh man.

We sit out here around the fire enjoying each other's company under the canopy of the midnight sky. I began to tell her I have never realized just how beautiful the midnight sky really is out here in the desert, for you can see all the beautiful stars that appear in heaven. When there is no other brighter lights to interfere with the light being brought forth by the stars of heaven, they are almost as beautiful as her; her beauty, in my eyes, outshine all other light that is known to mankind. I begin to tell her how much that I miss being home riding my motorcycle.

She asked, "Just what is a motorcycle?"

I tried to explain to her just what a motorcycle is.

She replied, "I have never seen such a machine as that in my country."

The fire is beginning to burn itself out, so we say good night, and she goes back to her tent and I go into mine and go to bed to rest this old body of mine. For if tomorrow's journey is going to be anything like today's was, I'm going to need all the rest I can get.

SWEET DREAM

As i sleep, I begin to dream about the day in which I find myself of begin out of this desert. I awake from my deep sleep only to find myself to be on my own once again in my life. Why? So I walk out of my tent only to discover that I am by some lake that appears to be on some deserted island, so I thought it was because there were no one around as far as I could see. I started to walk around the lake, listen-ing to the birds and the other animals that are in the woods making their joyful sound; it was like they were singing a song of praise unto our Lord. I continue walking farther into the woods. Just the smell coming from the flowers and honey-suckles was so refreshing to my senses. I found a place to sit down and enjoy all the sounds and smell that Mother Nature had for me. As I was sitting there, I begin to feel something rubbing up against my leg. It startled me; I did not know what it could have been out here in the wild, you know.

I slowly looked down trying not to startle whatever it might have be, Oh, it was just a camel licking my leg; it was just a dream. I get up and start taking down the tent and packing it away. We get all the tents down and packed away for our journey. As the caravan moved out, one of the camels trips and breaks its leg. It looks just like the one that woke me up from my dream of being out of this desert. We had to unload him and spread the load out unto the others before we could get on the move again. Now that we are down one camel, we can't move as fast as we did before. The camels that are way out in front of us seem to be coming to a halt for some reason, so we continue to move on up to see just why they are stopping. The leader of the caravan began to explain to me. If I was to continue traveling in the same direction that we were heading in, I would be in a half day of reaching the ocean. I'm now one happy man to hear these words, but I had to ask, what good would this do me?

A WAY OUT

He said if I went left or right, I would come to a small town that has boats bringing supplies from time to time into the town, for the people. One of the beautiful wildflowers and myself continue on our journey in the direction in which we was heading in, but we got there in half the time that he had said we would. As we come into the town, some people begin to come out to greet us and ask just where we come from. I try my very best to explain to them why we have come unto their town, but I am not having much luck in doing so, for I do not speak their language. For I have always heard ole saying, "If it was not for bad luck, I would have no luck at all." Well, that the way I'm feeling right now, but must I say, I am not going to give up, for I have traveled too far and too long to just quit now on my journey in getting out of this desert.

The day is fast coming to its end. We must find rooms to rest for the night and a place to eat dinner. We find a nice restaurant to have, and just as before, she come in to room dressed as beautiful as one can possibly get. As we sit at the table, we begin to discuss just how we are going to communicate with the people of this town, in explaining to them just what it is that we are looking for in getting out of this desert.

ONES PRAY

O Lord my God, hear my heart cry, for it feels as if it's going burst from the tear in which it's crying, for my heart can't hardly continue to beat from the tears that are flowing into my heart as if a rushing river is running into a small steam. As the tears flowed faster, it becomes that much harder to find within my flooded soul to describe my true feeling for such a lovely lady as the one whom is standing before me.

O Lord my God, do hear my cry? For I do not understand why such a lady as her has come across my path, for I have found myself falling for her beauty. Why that is, I do not know. What I do know is she has a way about her that keep me wanting to know everything about her.

O Lord, my cry out unto you on this great matter is unlike any other cry before. Lord, I don't know just how to explain why I am feeling the way I do for her, for I am such you know, Lord, the right way in which I should go with this situation I have found myself to be in, Lord. Lord my god, for everything that takes place here in our life, you do have a greater purpose. I may not understand it all now. I just ask for your will to be done. I know you do have everything in your control, my Lord. For I ask, Lord, if you don't have everything in your control then how could we all even breathe, taste, love, walk, talk, or even see without you being in control? For if she could just find it within her heart to forgive me for making such a mess of everything, I will try my very best to do things in a much better way than I did in the beginning of our friendship. I cannot make a promise that I will get it right every time, for after all I am just human and I do make mistakes, just as I know she does herself in her life. She is doing her best to make a life for herself and her family in this world we are living in. O Lord, she has given you the key to her heart to safeguard her loving heart for eternity. Just by her believing in you is the most wonderful thing a man like myself could ask for in a soul mate. She is one of a kind; someone like her is hard to find in today's journey of life. O Lord my God, I do pray that you will keep me on the path you have laid out before me to travel down. Now looking back into the living words of 1 Corinthians 7, I find that Paul had this to say, "Now concerning the things whereof ye wrote to me: it is good for a man not to touch a woman. Nevertheless, to avoid firnifi-cation let every man have his own wife and let every woman have her own husband, let the husband render unto the wife due be devouring braless and likewise also the wife unto the husband the wife having not power over her own body the husband and likewise also the hus-band having not power over his own body but the wife." Amen!

A PLAN OF ACTION

.

Now I am thinking we have come up with a good game plan on how we are going to communicate with the nice people of this town in which we are now in. Well, this it is not going to work either, for we cannot write the words that we need in their language. Now let's just see if this idea might work. She looks at me with those baby brown eyes of hers. Everything just went blank; her eyes put me into a trance that impaired my thinking. All I could think of at this moment was wanting her to open the door of her heart and allowing me to get to know more about her. O Lord, I ask for you to help me open the door to her heart and just let her love flow upon me like a stream of the living waters that I may drink from to quench the dying thirst that is within my soul, for her endless love flows from her divine loving heart for all eternity.

The night is now fast approaching us, and we have not yet found us a room. We need to find rooms for the night if I am to come up with a way to describe unto the people just what it is that we are looking for in order for them to help us to get out of this hot scorching desert. We go from one place to the next asking about a place that may have rooms for rent. We find ourselves having a hard time communicating with these nice people. I am thinking about looking for a bookstore that has books that may have pictures of what it is that we are looking for, and just maybe they can understand and be able to communicate in a much better way than what we are now. I hope by me showing them a picture of what we are looking for, just maybe by then it won't be too late, or we might have to find a stable to spend the night in just for tonight. We do find a bookstore, but you know what, if it was not for my bad luck, I would have no luck at all; the bookstore was closed for the night.

She looks at me once again with those eyes of hers, and I just had to look away from those eyes, for I had to think about what I was going to do next. I'm going to sleep here until morning. I do find in a book just what I'm looking for. I show it to a man, and he took us to the place where the boats were at, so my new journey will continue to go forward, unto where I don't know.

I asked the man who showed us just where the boats were to come in, and he held up three fingers. I was not sure just what it was that he was trying to tell us. I don't know if it was going to be three hours or three days. For I try to take a different approach on just how I'm asking him on what it is that I need to know. I look at my watch and decide if I could get him to understand me by pointing at the hour hand to see if it was three hours he was trying to tell us. I'm praying that this idea of mine will work for us. For I find within myself also asking in my prayers, Lord my God, why is this happening to us at that point in time?

THE VOICE OF REASON

heard a soft voice reply, "For your story tells who you were and as for what you have done, makes you who you are today, and just what you are going through will make you that much stronger. For I have been with you through it all, and I will continue to be with you through the end. All I am asking of you is to keep your faith in me." Now I show my watch to the man to see if he would understand what it is that I'm asked of him. He does understand this, but he gives me a sign as to say, "No, that is not what I was trying to tell you when I held up three fingers."

I turned to her, trying not to make eye contact with those baby brown eyes of hers, for they do hypnotize me in a way that I cannot think straight. I asked of her if she knew any words that she could speak in his language that would help us to ask for someone to translate what I'm asking him. She replied, "I will try my best, but I don't know much about their language."

She began to ask him if he knew anyone who might be able to help us to find out just when the supply boats are to be coming in. I think that he did understand. He began to take us to this house. He told her that there was someone he knew that lived there and would be able to help us. We finally get to this house. We knocked on the door, and an older gentleman answered the door. He greeted his friend with a kiss on the cheek and a hug, then he asked, "How can I be of help to you?"

I began to ask if he knew just the time the supply boats would be coming in.

He replied by holding up three fingers as to when the next shipment of supply boats would be coming back with more supply.

"What is with the three fingers," I asked.

THE LACK OF UNDERSTANDING

He began to say three weeks and three days ago, the boats brought in their supplies, and they only come every three months. I do the math. I'm going to be in this desert for lot longer than I had anticipated on being here. I have to look at the positive side of this situation. I'm at a place that has ships coming and going out, but most of all, I have with me one of the most beautiful wildflowers that one man such as I can be with. So with this in mind, just hopefully everything will work out for the best for the two us.

We need to find a place to stay in this desert town until the next shipment of supply are delivery. I ask this nice gentleman if he knew just where we might find such a place to stay until the next time the ships are to come in. He replied that we were more than welcome to stay with him and his family.

Little did I know just what a big family he had. The lady asked if they would excuse us, for we needed to talk this over with each other before we could give him our answer. He said, "Sure, take your time and talk it over and be sure that this is what you and your friend would like to do." We step to the side and began to talk it over, and we decide to try this for one or two nights. For we do not know of any other place that we could stay. We went back over to the gentle-man and gave him our answer; he invited us into his home and began to introduce us to all his family. He has three wives, and by the first wife, he has three daughters by, and the second three sons. As for the third wife, being the youngest of the three, she has just one daughters and one in the oven. As we sit around try our best to get acquainted, crazy old me asked a question. Now you must understand I'm not familiar with the custom of which these people live.

I ask, "How is it you have three wives and by these three wives one has three daughters and the second three sons, and for the third just one daughter?"

He looks at me as if he was going to ask me a question, but instead he replied, "For I'm a very rich and powerful man who owns a great of livestock that need attending every day. Therefore, I need many children to help take care of my great possession."

As we continue to try our best on communicating, he goes on and tells me that he also owns most of the ships that brings the supplies that helps to provide for the needs of the people that live in this desert town in which we are now in. He also stated not for these people that is living in this town, but also for the people who are living far out in the desert, for they are also in need of supplies if they are going to survive in this country.

I ask him about the other town, how the supply ship comes in and out of there, and if he knew just when was the last time they brought supplies in to that town? He tells me that they come and go just as they do here at this town, for the same ships that deliver our supplies also delivers them their supplies, but not at the same time. For they cannot haul that much supplies at one time.

THE MOVES OF SON

As he tells me all this, I catch a glimpse of one of his sons begin-ning to put the moves on the beautiful lady that is with me. I can no longer listen to him while watching his son trying to put the move on her. I don't know why this is getting to me like it is. I cannot even find the words within myself to tell her the way I'm beginning to have very strong feeling for her in such a way I have never felt for a beautiful woman as her in my entire life. There just something about her that makes me feel like life itself will go on for all eternity. When I'm in her sweet presence, nothing else in this world in which I'm living seems to matter to me as much as seeing the happiness shine on that extraordinary beautiful face of her.

I just would like to be able caress her beautiful, soft rosy cheeks and look into those baby brown eyes of her and say unto her, "I cannot promise you the world that you so greatly deserve, but I can promise you that I will do my very best to make the world in which you are living in a much lovely place for you. Oh, my heart is crying out for you to come and open the floodgates of my heart and let my love flow freely and find its way into your heart. Oh my sweet and lovely lady, I cannot find the right way unto your heart, for my heart itself appears to be drowning from the tears that is trying to find their way out unto you."

UNKNEW LOVE

Oh, once again I find myself asking how much longer I must go on without being able to just let my love show for such a beautiful lady as her. She must have her love locked up deeper than any man can go. As I sit here trying to figure out just what it is that makes her so difficult and complicated to figure out, I find myself going back to the beginning of my journey in this life just to see what it could be about myself that is keeping me from begin able to express just who I'm and how I truly feel about her. Well, let's just see, when I was just a newborn baby, begin born tongue-tied, the doctor clipped the part that had my tongue tied down, but as all babies do, as I grew, it grew back as well, making it difficult to learn how to pronounce certain words. I did not know all this about myself until I reached the age when I had to start school.

LEARNING ABOUT ONE'S SELF

Now my first year in school, I made As and Bs, so the first year was not all that bad. It was not obvious in my life that being tongue-tied was going to become such a challenge in my life. It did not make that much difference being born tongue-tied, for we all, at that age, had some of our baby teeth missing, making us all have some diffi-culty in making the proper sounds for some words. The first year of school was a great one, but all good things do come to its end. I got my report card, and it shows that I have pass to the second grade.

Well, school's out for the summer, and we all are enjoying our summer break, but during this summer break, something comes up with the home we are living, in and we have to move back to the place where I was born. Now this means having to leave my friends, all two of them, one of them being my girlfriend. Well, she is a girl, and she was my good friend also. It was a hard thing to do either way you look at it. To start a new school in which you do not know anyone is hard, let me tell you.

Now we are back to my first home. I'm looking back on my first childhood memories at this home, for it was a great place to live and is still to this day. There is one thing greatly different about this place, though, and that is Mom and Dad have gone on to be with our Heavenly Father.

Well, now I was about three years old now and was playing outside as all kids did back in those days; we did not have video games and cellphone to play with as kids do today. When your mom or dad told you to do something, you did just it, or you would most definitely regret not doing it when they told you. Now before I go any further, I need to clarify that my dad passed away when I was two years old, and as for mom, she passed away just a few years ago. As I was saying, I'm about three or four years old at this time.

We were outside playing in the driveway under an old blackjack tree that stood in the middle of the driveway. I was digging in the dirt. That's when my big toe got struck by a shovel, almost cutting it off. Well, I began to cry. Mom heard me. She and Grandma and Mom's sister came running out of the house to see just why I was crying. When they saw the blood coming from my foot, they snatched me up and started do everything that they could think of to get the bleeding to stop. One tore rags into and wrapped them around my toe. The best that I can recall, they may have even poured turpentine on the rags to help get the bleeding to stop. Then off to the doctor we go. I am still crying all the way to the doctor's office. The nurse took Mom and me back to the examination room, and Mom had to start filling out the paperwork that was needed to be filled out. Then the nurse started to take off the rags for the doctor to do what he needed to do---and that was save my toe. The best I can remember, he put seven stitches across the top of my toe. Why am I telling you this, one might ask. Well, I am trying to pass time until the supply ship comes back in.

As time goes by, I find myself back once again having to go to the doctor. I was playing chase with my brothers. I was running after one of them when I stepped on a cigarette butt that my uncle had thrown out the window. Well, it put a blister on the bottom of my foot. Being a kid, I didn't think anything about it. So one day we go swimming, the blister became infected, and I ended up being put into the hospital this time. In order for the doctor to give me something to fight the infection, they had to cut just above my ankle to give me the drip to fight the infection. The scar is still there to this day. Since I am talking about being in the hospital, I might as well go ahead and tell you it seems it wasn't long after that I had to have my tonsils taken out. Now that's the last time I can remember being in the hospital until later on in life.

A HARD LESSON LEARNED

Back to my second years in school. I must say I had some great teacher that year, for they knew just how to use a paddle. For They tore my butt up, for they used one many times on mine backside so they had a lot of practice with using one let me tell you. Now as I look back on all of this, I got to say, this was just some of my learning experience that helped me to become the person that I am today. My second year in school got a little bit harder, being unable to pro-nounce and spell bigger words. My grades began to decline, and all the other kids begin to make fun and pick on me because I was hav-ing a hard time keeping up with them in our classwork.

Well, the last nine-week test was upon us, and I was nervous about taking all the tests that we had to take, but I was able to pass all of them. The homeroom teacher gave out our report cards to take home and have our parents to sign and be returned back to the school. Well, where it says advance to the next level of learning, the teacher had put the number three there.

I take the report card home to show it to Mom for her to see and sign it. Back then, the school mailed out the report cards at the end of the school year. Therefore, it had to have an envelope with my home address on it. School was finally out for the summer, and I was one happy little boy because I was thinking that I had passed to the third grade, Well, we finally got our report cards in the mail. Mom opened the envelope and pulled the card out to look at it. Someone had used

Liquid Paper on the number three and put the number two in its place. You could still see the number three through the liquid paper.

Well, me and my brothers went on to enjoy our summer vacation for it was around this time that we were having our new home built. Being the kids that we were, we used the scrap panels as a slate to slide down a sawdust pile that we had found. There used to be and old sawmill about a mile up the road from where we were having our new home built.

As I look back on the days, they were some of the best days of my life as a young boy. Now it is time for school to start back. Mom takes me for the first day just to find out why I had to repeat the second grade. Mom confronts the principal and the teacher that I had the year prior with my report card. I thought that Mom was about to go to jail because she had come unglued on both of them because of what the teacher said. The teacher had blamed Mom and said she was the one who put the number three on my report card when she send it home with me. Therefore she used the Liquid Paper to white it out and put the number two in its spot.

Well, needless to say, I had to repeat the second grade over again, and you know what that does to a young boy's confidences and self-esteem? It had brought me down to a level that led me to withdraw myself from letting people get to know just who I am. Even to this day, I find it hard to get close to people because of my past experience with people making fun of my inability to pronounce certain words. Why do I say this, you may ask yourself. Because still to this day, I feel I don't fit in because of my inability to learn things like others do. I feel as if people still look down on me for not being as smart as they are and not being able to read and write like everyone else. Well, there are some friends I have asked to read some of what I have written up to this point, and they would ask, "Did you write this? This is a side of you we never knew of, a side that you have never let be known."

Now that I have started writing my own book, people have come to realize there is a side to me they never knew. So, see, this is just some of the reasons I have withdrawn myself from others and stopped letting people get to know the real me. With that being said, just forgive me for my imperfection as God has forgiven you and love me for who I am. Try not changing me for God has already molded me just the way he wants me to be as he has you. I repeated the second grade, but this time they put me with a teacher who has a teacher helper, who is someone who could help you if you needed extra help with your classroom work.

As the school year continues to move forward, I find myself car-rying home some papers that the teacher has given me to take home to Mom to fill out and be returned to the teacher. Well, little did I know at that time, these papers was for them to give me a special test to find out if I had a learning disability. If you have read up to this point, the only problem I do have is with proper pronunciation of words, and that is from being born tongue-tied. Mom signs the papers, and I take them back and give them to my teacher. She sent the paper to wherever they had to go to be approved. By this time, school was almost over for the year, and I did pass to the third grade. Now the papers do get approved for this test that they need me to take.

While on our summer break, we get a visit from this lady who wanted to take me to the school to take this test. Mom has me to get cleaned up and go with this lady to take the test. Well, I must not have passed the test for they put me in this class for slow-learning students. There were between just maybe ten or fifteen others in this class. Well, school has not yet started, so we are out cleaning up from where we had torn down our old house. As we boys would move the old lumber, Mom would cut the grass where the lumber had been. Well, somehow Mom got a big splinter stuck through the top of her foot. She goes into the house where my stepdad was at the time to see if he would pull it out. He take one look and says, "Baby, I will not try to pull that out of your foot. You are going to the doctor to have it cut out."

So Mom and my two younger sister gets in the truck, and we four boys, well, we get on the back of the truck, and we are now headed to the doctor's office. We got about halfway there when this other vehicle lost control and hit us on the driver's side, throwing us into a spin that threw my baby brother and myself off the back of the truck. The two oldest, they saw it coming and jumped off, not getting hurt that much. As for my baby brother, he suffered a severe concussion, and the baby girl, she also had a severe concussion and had to be airlifted to the hospital. As for my other sister, I not just sure what injuries she received from the wreck. Now Mom got the left side of her head split open. Mom told us as she was lying on the examination bed that Dad stood beside her and said these words, "Baby I love you," and that he also said, "Take care of our children for I'm gone on to be with the Lord."

A SINGLE PARENT

Now dad, he was a good-size man, but the impact from the two vehicles colliding was so great that it drove the steering wheel column into him. He later died that day from the injuries that he received. For I did not know all that had took place until I came to in the hospital and looked over at my oldest brother, and I said unto him, "Daddy is dead, is he not?" He began to tell me with tears in his eyes just what had happened that sad and unforgettable day in our lives, for we had not only lost our dad that day, we also lost a great man who loved us boys as if we were his very own flesh and blood. Still to this day, I hold in my heart many great memories of him. I'm going to share just one with you.

I was about five years old at this time. He was sitting at the dinner table drinking a cup of coffee, and I asked if I could have some of his coffee. He gave me some, and I accidentally spilled it, so he sent me to get the mop from off the back porch to clean it up. Well, as I started back in with mop, Mom's cat started in also, but the door shut on the cat's tail, and let me tell you, that cat let out a scream that made the hair on my head stand straight up. I was frozen at that moment in time, for I did not know just what had come in through that door be behind me. He and my brothers was laughing so hard at me that they were rolling on the floor.

Now once again, Mom finds herself having to take care of not just four boys but also two girls all by herself. Well, it is almost time for school to start back, and Mom is doing all she can to get us four boys new clothes and shoes, notebook, paper---everything that one would need for school, but being a single mom who did not have much of an income coming in, it was pretty hard to provide all that one would need for school, but we were happy to have all that we did have at that time. We knew just what was going on in our life at the time. So what if we didn't have a twenty-five-dollar pair of shoes or some name-brand shirt or pants that cost thirty or forty dollars to wear to school? The clothes or shoes that you wear do not help teach you the true value of love and respect for other. Before I go down to the shoreline to see if the ships are within sight, I would like to tell you just one shorter story that I remember about my stepdad.

LONELY MEMORIES

The Home That we once lived in was not a very big house; it had just two bedrooms, a living room, and the kitchen. You then had the front and back porch, and that was it. We did not have indoor plumbing at this time. The story goes that he had to go out to the outhouse that night. I was in bed and was looking out the window, and all at once, he comes up from under the window with a sheet over his head.

Boy, let me tell you, this little boy dove under the sheets. I could not say anything. I was shaking. My brother asked, "What is wrong with you?"

All I could do is point to the window. About that time, Dad came back in the house with the sheet in his hand and a smile on his face, and said, "Son, you look like if you had just seen a ghost. Did it look just like this?" He held up the sheet.

He only whipped me once, and I not going to say why he did, but after that one whooping, he never had to do it again. That whooping taught me a lesson I would never forget, let me tell you.

Now as for Mom, I'm surprised that I'm not still carrying the stripes of a zebra. I'm not saying that I didn't need them. I'm pretty sure I did need them, and then some. Forever I will love you always, Mom and Dad, for the man you have taught me to become in this life's journey that our Heavenly Father has placed before me.

OVERLOOKING THE OCEAN

Now i find myself to be down at the ocean looking out across the water to see if I can spot any of the supply ships out on the horizon of the ocean. No, not one do I see coming at this time. Now I'm feel-ing somewhat down and discouraged about this journey that I have found myself to be on, for I am finding it to be one of the hardest roads to travel down out of the others that I have traveled. I do know that at any time, I can go unto my Heavenly Farther and ask for his help to calm the storm that I have found myself to be in.

LOST OF LOVE

One of the hardest days in my life was when I came home from work, and the one person I had devoted my entire life in loving and caring for told me on my birthday that she no longer loved me as she once did. I'm like, "What is up with you, and why are you saying these things unto me today of all days, it being my birthday."

Well, we stayed married for another year, and it was a couple months until our divorce became final. Now you know why I have found myself to be on this journey of life as a free and single man once again. For I'm looking forward to the day in which the supply ships will arrive once again, for my journey must move on down this ole rugged road of life in search of my beautiful soul mate, for I feel that she is also out there somewhere in this old world just waiting for my arrival, just when that will be, I don't know, for now it seems to be impossible for me to find my way unto her.

As I sit here alone looking out across the crystal clear blue ocean, I'm reminded of a time when my stepdad took us to a river that had a place where you could go in swimming. I was just a very young boy who had not learned how to swim. Well, we all go in the water, and as I go in, the water kept getting deeper, and I found myself crawling up my stepsister's back. We both almost drowned that day, and because of that day, I'm not that fond of water; therefore, I'm praying that the ship I get on to leave this desert does not spring a big leak.

ONE'S FEELS COME AND GO'S

As I'm sitting here pondering my thoughts on just where this journey of mine may take me next, I hear the waves of the ocean as they are coming in and or going back out. They remind me of one's feeling for they also come and go, and just where they go nobody knows for certain. The feeling I once had for the most beautiful lady that was with me on this journey of life has become like the waves of the ocean, just where they went I don't know.

Now as my journey continues to go forward, I find that the feeling I once had for this beautiful wildflower, has become also like unto the wavers of ocean. Could it be just why I'm feeling this is that I'm unable to express unto her in the way I would love to able to win over her broken heart? For all I can do now is just hope and pray that if it would be in God's will for her to open up the door of her heart and just let me try my best to be a friend unto her, someone she can talk to about anything that is on her mind, like how her day at work went or how she is feeling.

As I am walking along the oceanfront, I'm feeling that she is starting to have feelings for one of the older gentleman sons because she is being much friendlier with him than she was with me in the beginning, but only time will tell the truth about their relationship. Will she continue this journey we have started together from the time in which we became acquainted the day they found me about dead in this desert?

SUN STARTS TO DESCENT

The sun starts its descent to close out this beautiful day our Heavenly Father has so blessed us with. Now I have found myself to have walked a great distance from where I had started. I must stop here and head back in the same direction in which I came from. I'm not for sure if that I'm going to make it all the way back before the sun has closed out this lovely day. If I don't, the light from the moon and stars that shine ever so brightly from the beautiful heavenly skies will surely be my guide back to where I came. The light from the sweet midnight moon and stars are so bright out here in this desert; it provides me with the light to see my way.

I continue to walk. I look out upon the ocean. The moonlight reflecting upon the crystal clear ocean, oh, it is just so beautiful and peaceful. I could just lay down right here and try counting the stars of heaven as I listen to the sound of the waves come and go. It as if they are trying to tell me a story of a love that is awaiting me somewhere out in this big old world, but just where they don't know. As I continue to make my way back to the house by the light of the moon, I see in the far distance what appears to be two shadows out walking by the moonlight also. For the life of me, I cannot help but think just maybe that it could be the son and the wildflower that is with me on this journey out of this desert. As I do get closer to the house, I see someone sitting on the steps. It is her, so I also sit down beside her. As for the two I saw, they just kept on walking, unto where I do not know. Now we just sit here in the lovely moonlight, and from right out of the blue, she asks, "Why did you leave me here all alone?" Why didn't I ask her if she wanted to go with me?

Now I'm thinking, *Now is this not just like a beautiful woman?*

"What, did you not stop and think that I too would have loved to have taken a walk in the moonlight and seen the lovely reflection of the moon and stars upon the clean blue ocean? I have only dreamed of seeing such beauty."

ROMANTIC THOUGHT IN TIME

The way she asked me this brought tears into my eyes, and I could not find the words to answer her at that moment because of the tears and the big lump in my throat. When I was able to answer her, it was like a light came on within my heart. For the first time in my life, I found the words within my soul to say unto this beautiful and lovely lady and express the way I was beginning to have feeling for her unlike what I have ever had before for a woman.

She looks at me with those baby brown eyes of hers and says, "I had no clue that you were starting to feel this way about me."

I am thinking, *Is this not typical of a woman?*

A MOONLIGHT WALK

Then she asked, "Could we go for a walk down by the ocean? For I would love to see just how beautiful the ocean is by the moonlight."

I was somewhat shocked by her response to what had told her, but nevertheless I responded back, "Yes, I would love to take a walk with you down by the oceanfront," if it would make her heart happy and bring back that beautiful adorable smile upon her face. As we made our way to the ocean, neither her or myself said a word to each other; we just walked and listened to the waves of the ocean as they came in and went back out.

As we continue, she begins to sing a song unlike any other song I had ever heard before. It was a beautiful and powerful song. When she has finished her song, I asked her, "Where did you learn such a beautiful song as that one?"

She replied, "My mom sang it to me once in my dream that I had once about a night such as this one." She when on telling me about how this night reminded her so much of that dream she once had about her mother singing this song. "And that is why I have sung it tonight for you."

MIXED SIGNALS

I find within myself once again just wanting to reach out to her and take her into my arms and hold her for all eternity, but I keep feeling that she is sending mixed signals, leaving me in a eunuch state of mind, not knowing just what it is that I was supposed to do in my journey with her. There are time like tonight that she will talk with me about some things, and then there's time in which she will just say one or two words to me. I know that she has her work and all, and that's okay, but one does need time for oneself sometime. Maybe one day I will get this figured out before I die, or maybe not only time will tell in the end. But until I do, I must continue in this journey of life not knowing for certain just where I may end up in this life of my, in which our Heavenly Father has put me on to travel. All I know is to give him all my praise each day, for it is he that gives me the breath to live by.

It has gotten late, and we have walked quite a great distance along the ocean. We must return to the house for the remainder of the night. Now the breeze that is coming from off the ocean has gotten mighty cool for this old country boy. She is just as lovely in the moonlight as she is in the light of day. One can only wonder if our friendship will grow in time or if it will become like the waves of the ocean, for they come in and they go back out, unto just where no will ever know for certain. Only she knows for it is she that holds the true answer to this question. I only know God holds the only key to the door of her beloved heart. Only she can open it from within to be a true and faithful friend with someone of her own choosing.

THE SONG OF POWER

As we begin to make our way back to the house, I asked of her if she would mind singing that beautiful and so powerful song of her. Now as she began singing her song, the waves of the ocean seemed to rise and stop in midair, as if they themselves were listening to her sing this beautiful and powerful song. When she had finished singing her song, the waves of this ocean just fell and went back out, unto where one can only dream of ever knowing.

I find myself asking her once again more about this song. This time, she explained in much greater detail that it was about when our Savior, Jesus, was pierced in his side by a Roman soldier that day in which he hung upon that ole rugged cross, and from his side there came flowing down his own blood and water. I then ask her, "What is the title of this song?"

She replied, "I do not know if it has a title or not. I guess," she says, "one could title it as 'The Amazing Power of the Blood and Water.'" By now we have made our way to the house, and as we make our way unto our rooms, we say one to the other good night and sweet dreams.

I in my room getting ready to lie down to sleep, but before I do just that, I must first say my prayers unto our Lord, thanking him for each and every blessing that he has bestowed upon me this great day. I must say, the greatest blessing was his son's blood that washed away my sins that day his blood came flowing down that old rugged cross.

I find myself asking in my prayer if he would show me a way to express unto her how I would so much for us to become friends. That night in my sleep, it did come unto me by way of a beautiful, sweet dream. Only time will tell if it will work or not.

Well, just like always, I start my day off with my most favorite drink of the day, and that would be a big cup of black coffee. Would anyone else like to have a cup? No, oh well, just thought I would ask.

MY MORNING COFFEE

As I sit here drinking my cup of coffee, I'm in deep thought about the dream I had last night, for here I'm in this old desert, and just where to go looking for what I'm needing to show this lovely wild-flower that I'm now find myself with feelings for her, that I'm serious about wanting to be a part of her life. One can only dream of having such happiness in their lifetime when they are with the one who keeps their heart beating with endless love, just knowing that at the end of your hardest day, that one love will always be there for you in the good and worst times in your life.

Now as I start on my journey in this town in search of what I hope will represent the beginning of a friendship with her, I come across a store with some motorcycles. I go in and just started looking around at the different styles that they had in the store. As I'm looking around, there came up a much older gentleman who said, "May I help you, sir?"

I started looking around to see just who he was speaking to. I didn't see anyone, so I looked back and said, "Who me?"

He said, "Yes, you do you see anyone else? Now do you need help with something?"

I replied, "Well, no, sir, I'm was just admiring the bike you have here. They remind me when I was just a young boy growing up, as to when I got my first bike."

GOOD OLD DAYS

Looking back once more in to my childhood memories, that bike was giving to me by one of my mom's first cousin. It was a very old bike that did not run; therefore, we would push one another on it wherever we wanted to go on it. Well, one day we were outside playing on it, for across the road in front of the house was at one time an open field with some rows; that is where we would play rid-ing the bike. We would push each other across the rows, using them as a ramp. Well, this one day as we were playing on it, and this day became the last day for this old bike that we all came to love and had some much fun on just pushing each other around. We were pushing one of my cousins on it, and he jumped on to many of the terraced rows. He and the bike came down into a pine tree, bending the han-dlebar and the front wheel of the bike, putting an end to its use for fun, and oh, what fun it was.

Now we are back playing cowboys and Indians with a stick for our horses and homemade bow and arrows. We would make our bows out of vines that we found growing along the side of an oak tree out in the woods behind the house. When we found a good vine that we could use, we would cut it to the length we needed and then cut a slots on each end for the nylon string that we use to shoot the arrows with. As for the cowboys, they would use homemade slingshots; that was their choice of weapon. Now we made them from a small forked limb with a piece of rubber tied to each fork of the limb with a piece of leather fastening them together, using a rock or whatever we could find to use as our ammunition.

If we weren't playing cowboys and Indians, we were out riding our bicycles. We would find an old bike that wasn't any good and cut the front forks off and slide them upon forks of the good bike, making it into a chopper. Back when I was growing up as a young boy, it was hard to come up with any extra money to buy any toys to play with when there are four boys and two girls. Therefore, we used whatever we could find to play. Well, one day I found an old bike, and I cut the forks off it and put them on my bike. At that time, we had no good way to keep them from coming back off. They would come off from time to time, more so when you would be popped a wheelie. Back then boys' and girls' bicycles had what we called banana seats, the reason being they looked just like a banana, long and had a curved at the end. Well, the gravel dirt road that ran in front of our home about hundred yards or so was a covered that had a hold almost on one end. As I was riding my new chopper that I just made, I came upon the hole in the covered. Well, crazy me went to pop a wheelie to miss the hole, not thinking about what would happened if the forks was to come off. Well, they came off. When I came back down over the handlebars, I went face-first into gravel. Oh no, it didn't hurt at all. I just picked up the forks and wheel and put them back on and went on riding as if it never happened.

As time went on, Mom, she remarried. I'm much older now and able to help cut grass for our neighbors during the summer time. I could save up some money to buy a horse from one of my friend that I went to school with. Well, as one may know, when one child gets something, the other wants one also, so mom goes and buys him one as well. Now my horse does not like his horse; he tried to hurt him time after time.

One day as we are coming home from school, we passed this pickup with a horse trailer behind it. They got rid of my horse. Well, as time went on, my next oldest brother goes and buy him a horse; he was male horse. One of our neighbors that I cut grass for, she had an old female horse, and when it came that time, well, you know, my brother's horse would jump the fence and go and try to make him a visit. Therefore we would go get him. This one particular time, me and my brother had to go get him, my brother was riding him, and I was on his horse, and he gets the bigger horse running. The one I was on started to run also. For the life of me, I don't know how I ended up under the horse's neck, holding on for dear life. I was calling out to him to get these horses to stop running. He was laughing so hard at me, he himself almost fell off before he got them stop. I just wanted to hurt him so bad for doing that to me, but all I could do was to laugh also, for I could picture that in my mind just how funny that must have looked. He looks at me as I'm telling him all this and just asks, "Would you like a cup of coffee?"

I replied, "Yes sir, I would at that."

He gets up and goes to get us the coffee. I look out the window and see two people walking down the sidewalk. One of them is her. The gentleman that's with her, I have not seen before. He come back with our cup of coffee, and we sit back down at the table. I began to talk about a time when I was still just a young boy.

FIRST VACATION

It was back during the summertime. My brother and I went and spent the summer with our uncle and his wife. They had a fish pond out back of their house and an old barn out to the side. Well, my uncle's wife had some friends that would come over from time to time and bring their boys and girls over, and we would go fishing and playing in the old barn when they would come over. It just so happens that one of the young ladies was around my age. She was a pretty lady, and we began to take a liking to each other. We would play together or just sit in the swing on the front porch and just hold each other's hand and talk as if we were all grown up.

Well one day my uncle's wife decided that we were going to visit them at their house, so we go to their home. Just like always, they sent us out to play in the yard. She and I were together, talking out by the side of the house, when this crazy little brother of mine comes up and began to tell her that the next time they come for a visit us at my uncle's house, that I wanted to take her out to the old barn, just the two of us, and do our own playing. Well, I guess her sister must have overheard him telling her this. She goes back and tells her mom and dad all that he had said. She supposedly thinks that I put him up to tell her this; therefore, she calls her and myself into the house and began to question me about this.

My reply is, "Ma, I didn't not say those things. Nor did I put him up to ask your daughter to go out to the barn with me."

I am thinking that she didn't like my answer for she also calls my crazy little brother who got this started in the first place in and questioned him about what he had said to her daughter. He answered her, "Well, I heard someone say if was him, he would ask her to go out to the old barn and play."

Needless to say, the next time they came over to my uncle's house, there was no more going out to the barn and playing or fishing for the two of us; someone had to be around us when we were together. All we could do was just sit in the swing on the front porch and hold each other's hands. Thanks, lil bro, for your great help that summer.

Well, time came for us to go back home for school was to start and we needed to buy new clothes. Oh, I'm sorry, you don't know what I mean when I said "excited." Well, it just means other things that one might would need for school are in life itself. Now as for the young lady that I had met that summer, we didn't get to see one another that much afterward, and I can barely remember see her sweet face.

SCHOOL DAYS MEMORIES

Well, school has started, and about two or three weeks into this school year, a new family moved into the area and started school with us. Oh my goodness, let me tell you, they had one daughter who I thought at that time was the most gorgeous young lady I had ever seen around this school. I'm not saying that the others look bad or anything, but to my eyes, she was the best-looking one of them all. I think her mom may have had a friend who was a teacher or someone who just may have work at the school. During recess, she would go to this one classroom and just spend time with this person. Well, one of my friends and I would go to the window and talk with this pretty young lady. She did this the entire school year. This being her first year at this school and not knowing that many people here, I'm thinking maybe that's why she could be going this person's class-room. One day as we were talking, I came right out and told her that I like her a lot and I think she is a very beautiful young lady. Okay, now she knows that I like her. She never said anything about how she may have felt toward me, but she did one day write upon the chalk-board that she liked my friend. But I didn't give up that easily; I kept on chasing after this lovely young lady until our sophomore year.

Now let me see here, I'm thinking it was our freshman year that the school could hire some students for the summer to help with school maintenance. I applied for the job and got it, along with her and other friends. The only way I had to go was on my motorcycle that Mom got me that summer. It was not a very big bike, but I rode that bike every day to my job that summer. It was a Honda XL 100 which is a very small bike.

After work, we would go down the swim hole where everyone hung out. She would go with us from time to time. Well, like I said, I didn't get her as a girlfriend. I did finally give up and move on to next journey of my life. There was this one young wildflower—no, I'm not going tell about her. I will tell you this one.

It was during the summer, and I was cutting grass for this man. One of his wife's friend came over with her daughter, who didn't look bad. She sees my motorcycle and asks if she could ride it to the end of the driveway, which was about a mile or so long. I'm standing here in deep thought, thinking about letting her ride my motorcycle. I guess it is okay just this once. She gets on it, and off she goes—now just hold on! I'm going to get to the not-so-good part. He looks at me and asks, "Would you like something stronger than a cup of coffee?

"No, thank you, sir," I reply, "but I would love a cup of coffee if you don't mind."

He gets up and goes get myself a cup of coffee. Now I don't know just what he had in his cup. I'm thinking if she has not made it back by the time I'm done drinking my coffee, I will go looking for her. Well, she has not come back, so I tell him I'm going out looking for her.

I find her at the end of the driveway. She had let it go dead, and she could not get it started again, so I get it started, and she wanted to drive it back. Once again I find myself thinking about this, a pretty girl driving my motorcycle with me behind her. Get your mind out of the gutter and don't even think that way! Okay, off we go! About halfway, the not-so-good part takes place. Oh yes, we wreck and twist the handlebars and busted the headlight and the front fender. I get up and make sure she's okay. I get the bike up and look it over and try straighten the handlebars back the best that I could. We still needed to get back to the house, but this time, I would be doing the driving. We make it back, and she now blames me for her wrecking my motorcycle. The only thing that I'm guilty of is getting on the back of my own bike with a girl driving it. That is my story about letting a girl ride my bike, and I'm sticking to just that.

SEARCHING FOR
THREE ITEMS

thank you for listening to my story, but it is getting late, and I must go on looking for what I have set out to find. If I can find such a thing in this desert to shown this lovely wildflower just how I feel about us becoming friends. It has gotten late now, so I will try again tomorrow. Good night and may God watch over you.

The night has come and gone. A new day begins as they always do, with a big cup of coffee, but as I pour myself a cup, I reminded of two things, the first being the older gentleman asking me if I needed something stronger than a cup of his coffee and the other being I saw her walking with another gentleman. The way yesterday went and the way I'm feeling right now about all that has taken place, I'm now thinking I just might need to go back and see if the older gentleman still has something stronger than this coffee that I'm drinking. I'm beginning to wonder if it would be worth my time and effort trying to be even friends with her at this point.

Now I have found myself asking, should I still go out in this desert town and try to find just the things that came to me in my dream that night not so long ago? I will for now continue to look for these things, although I'm starting to feel within my heart that she may not be the one who is to get them. They just may be meant for someone else that I will meet along the way in my journey in search of my beautiful wildflower. If I can find these three items in this town, I going to present them to her just to see what kind of response she will give me.

Now that I have finished my third cup of coffee, I'm going for a walk along the oceanfront. As I stand here just looking out across the ocean, I see what appears to be a large vessel headed into the shore.

I continue to walk along the oceanfront to where the ships come in just to see for sure what it is coming in, for one's eyes can play tricks on you after you have been out here in this desert for a long time.

"THE SHIP ARE COMING" "SEE A SHIP"

I walk to the dock and asked one of the gentleman that works there if that a ship I see headed toward us. He replied, "Let me take a look and see." He reaches over and picks up a big pair of binoculars and looks out across the water. As he is looking out over the ocean, I tell him that I have been waiting for this day to come for a long time now. When he had finished scanning the ocean with his binoculars, he turns to me and says, "Yes, it is vessel, but I must tell you that they are still about three days out from making it here to the dock,"

Well, once again crazy old me had to just go and ask, "How do you know this?"

He looks at me with a big grin on his face and said, "Young man, I have been doing this for a lot longer that you have been alive." I then replied to him, "Maybe so, but that does not answer my question as to how do you know this to be true. Okay, it is apparent you're not going to tell me, nor do I know if you ever will. I will tell you one thing for sure, this old boy is going to be here when that vessel does come in to make their delivery of supplies."

I head back to see if I could find her and let her know the great news about the ships that would be coming in about three days or so. I continue my way back.

I find myself thinking, *This does not give me much time to find the three items I'm have been looking for. Do I continue to try finding them or not?*

HEAR THE WAVES

This is why I am asking, do you recall me telling you about that time I took a walk alone down by the ocean and I said I heard the waves coming in and going out, and it was like they were trying to tell me of a love that is waiting for me somewhere out there in this old world, just where they didn't know? As I make my way back to the house, I heard the waves as they came in and went out. They reminded me of that night not so long ago when we took a walk in the moonlight and she sang that beautiful song of hers as we walked along the oceanfront. It was that very night the dream came unto me, showing me away unto her heart. And now I find myself becoming more confused than I have ever been in a very long time about what I should do. Do I just wait and see if she's still going to continue our journey together out of this desert? Oh well, I do have three or so more days to think this over before the vessel get here, and who knows just how long it will be before they go back out?

Well, I made it back to see if she is here at the house. I asked one of the daughters if she has seen her. She replied, "Yes, she went into town with Mother to do some shopping."

Well, do you know just how long they been gone?" I ask.

"Oh about an hour or so, I think."

"Okay, thanks."

A NEW STORE

head out to town also. As I come into town, I go by this store that has some small cars unlike I have seen before, so I stop and check them out. There so many different shapes and sizes and different color of these vehicles. They remind me back when we had goat car we would drive up and down dirt road as if we were all grown up. Mom would not let us take it out on the highway. If we were to go play with our friends, we had to stay on the dirt road with it at all time. One of our friends was the boy I told you about earlier that the young lady said she like.

I leave this store to continue my search for her. I guess by me being all excited about the ships that are coming in, I forgot to ask what it was that they came into town for. It would help me to know just where to look for them. The people are very friendly. I don't know if it's because they have never met someone from another country or it's just that they don't understand my language either. Well, it doesn't matter. They do listen as if they do understand, unlike some people who just look down their nose at you as if you are the most uneducated person in this world, without stopping and looking at their own imperfections; there some that may not know just what this word means. Just because someone is unable to pronounce certain words in properly does not mean that the person is uneducated, so don't underestimate that person for he or she may know more than you think they know.

SEARCHING FOR HER

I continue my walk in search for her. I find myself become hungry. I smell something that reminds me of food cooking. I'm hoping to find her first, but if not, oh well, I hope to find the food to be nearby. It is smelling so good right now. I said the people here are nice, well, so is the food. I did find the food first. They had some mixed vegetables, and I do believe he said that the meat was lamb chop. I don't know just what kind of seasoning they use on their food to get it to taste as good as it does. As I'm sitting here eating, up they walk, her and the older gentleman's wife and son. They sit down and order a four-course meal as well. As we sit here waiting on their food, I begin to tell her that I had taken a walk down by the ocean, and as I was walking, I looked upon the ocean only to see what appears to be a vessel headed in our direction, so I walk down to the dock to talk with one of the workers to see if he might be able to verify if what I saw was a vessel coming in our direction. Before I could tell her, she asked what his answer was.

So I told them that he said it is a vessel, but it will be about three days or so before it will make it to the dock. Now they have finished their meal, and they are ready to get back to their shopping. With everything I have seen take place with her and this other man from the time that we arrived here in this town, I'm not sure now if she is worth my time and efforts in trying any longer, but what I just can't get out of my mind is that one day when she had walked by me; it was as if she had hit me in the gut, taking my breath away. I could not take my eyes off her when she was in my presence, and that is the very reason I have asked my Lord why has this lovely wildflower of a lady came into my life journey. God, only you know the true answer to this question of mine heart, Lord. I know that I can put this all into your hands and let you be my heart guide on just which way I should go in this matter from this day forth.

WILL I FIND THEM OR NOT

As for now, I will continue my search for the three items that came unto me by way of a sweet, lovely dream that night. I get up and get going, where I don't know. I feel that I have been to just about all the stores in this desert town looking for them. Will I find them or not? That I don't know for my time is running out? As I start my walk back to the house, I come back up to the store where the motorcycle was, and I remember the conversation that I had with him earlier this week about my motorcycle, so I go in to see if he has any three wheels or any mini bikes. As I'm waiting for him to come out, I go looking around the store. He comes in and sees me and asks, "How are you today, my friend?"

"I'm doing okay, just feeling down about something."

He asks, "Would you like to talk about it? I got coffee, and I do still have something stronger if need be."

"No, sir, just coffee will be okay for now."

So he goes and gets us a cup, and we begin to talk.

I ask him if he remembers the three wheels or mini bikes.

"Yes, I do remember the three wheels. I have some over at my other store, but as for the mini bikes, I do not know just what they are."

I begin to describe just what a mini bike is. It a small two-wheel bike with a lawn mower motor on it. I begin telling him about the time my youngest brother had a three-wheel. We would ride it around the neighbor's house and ride in their fields just to jump rows. Now that was fun but also dangerous as well.

Well, he asks, "Did you ever find what you have be looking for?"

"No, sir," I replied. "I don't know just where I might would find a yellow and red rose."

He asked why a yellow and red rose.

I replied, "To let her know just how much her friendship really means to me."

"Okay, just what is the third item you were speaking of?"

THE FIRST NOTE

Well, as for the third, it is a note explaining to her what the yellow and red rose represents. The note may or may not read as follows: 'I would like to show you my thanks and gratitude for you taking time out of your busy schedule to read over a small part of my writing, for I know you have very little free time of your own to do the things that you would love to be doing with your family and friends. For the yellow rose that is before you represent what may be the beginning of a friendship. As for the red rose, it represents how one would feel towards their friend. For I know that God holds the only key to the door of your heart. For only you can open it from within to be friends with someone of your only choosing. I must ask, Will our friendship grow, or will it be like unto the waves of the ocean; for they come in, and they go out, unto where no one knows for certain? For only you know, for only you hold the answer to what could be the beginning of a very beautiful friendship as our lives move forward. For all I know is what you have told me in our very first conversation. As far as your story goes, you only told me just a small part of it. Whatever you have done in the past is your business, not mine. Whatever you are going through, I can only sympathize with you, for I myself have been done somewhat the same way by the one I thought was to be for life. There's just one more thing, you ask me if I would take you with me on this journey of mine? Now the time has come for us to depart this desert, and I'm going to ask you, are you going to go with me, or you going to stay?

I will say this, if you decide to stay or go, I say unto you just love yourself as you are. For God has already molded you just the way he wants you, as he has me. With this being said, let's try not to change each other, but just love each other as we are. God has forgiven us for our failures, and he loves us as we are, so I ask just why can't we forgive each other?'"

He looks over at me and says, "Son, that was very nice. How about a cup of coffee?"

"Sure," I reply, "I would love a cup."

He come back with the coffee and asks, "Now is that the way your note to her is going to read?"

"I'm not sure if it is or not."

HIS FIRST LOVE

Well as we sit here drinking our coffee, I have forgotten just how many cups we have had, I ask him about his wife and how he met her. He began to tell me about his first love. "She was one of the most beautiful wildflowers that my eyes ever beheld. Looking into her eyes was like checking into heaven and seeing the streets made of gold, and her smile was like the pearly gates leaves into our Father's mansion. The only way to her heart would be by her opening the door from within, for she had given the key of her heart to God also, to safeguard from any intruders that may bring any heartache to her already fragile heart."

I asked, "Did she ever open the door and let you get to known her?"

He replies, "Yes, she did, and we got married and had two beau-tiful children together. She was about midway with the third child when she began to have some complications that took both of them out of this world."

"I'm very sorry for your loss, sir."

"Thank you, for she was one of a kind, unlike any other I have ever met in my life."

"Sir, may I ask just how did you ever get her to open the door from within her heart to you?"

He looks at me and said, "Son, I did something like you are doing now, but I did just two things a little different. I just waited with time and patience for if she is the right one, she will come around and open the door from within her heart unto you in her time. You talk as if you have some strong feeling for this lovely lady that you have come across in this desert."

"Yes, sir. You are right about this, but there is just one thing different here. In my situation, my time here in this small town in this desert with her is about to run out. What I'm saying here is that the ships are about to come in. I don't know if I'm going to be able to find those three items, and if I was to find them and give them to her, would I have the time to wait?"

He begins to tell me, "You do know the ships do come every three months, right? You do want her to open the door of her heart unto you?"

"Yes, you're right."

"Well now, what are you going to do?" he asks.

I asked just where in this town I could find the items I needed. He replied, "You might find them in the next town, for I don't

know of any store here that might have them." He went on to say that I could borrow one of his motorcycle to go into the next town to look for the items. By the time he had said all this and then some, all I could say was, "May I use your restroom? I must go from all the coffee that I have been drinking this morning, for it has got go somewhere."

He just chuckles and says, "Sure, go ahead. It's just down the hall the first door on your left."

I come back, and he asked, "Now would you like something stronger then coffee?"

I replied, "Sir, that is very thoughtful of you to ask, but I must say 'no, thank you.' I have seen firsthand as a child just what having a stronger drink can do to a person. I will just stay with my coffee for now, thank you. For now, I just need more time to think all this over before I decide on just what I going to do."

"Yes, you do," he replied.

"Sir, thank you for your time today. I will get back with you tomorrow on my decision."

TIME TO MAKE DECISION

'm going for a walk down to ocean. As I do, I begin to think about everything what he had said unto me this day, for it did make sense unto me. The way his first love turned out for him, and as for the ships, they do come in every three months. I am feeling that he is trying his very best to convince me that I should go into the next town and find these items and just give it a chance to work out and see if she will open the door of her beautiful heart.

As I continue my walk along the oceanfront, For I'm in deep thought about everything that has taken place into consideration. I find myself reflecting back in time to what, I have seen and heard things that, I now wish I had not seen or heard. Now I find myself feeling sad now, and I start to think that she is just half the lovely wildflower that I once believed her to be in the beginning of our journey out of this desert, in which I find myself.

Now once again I find myself needing to just take this unto my Lord, for he knows just what his will is for me and knows what I need when I need it.

I go unto my Lord and ask of him, "If it is not of your will for us becoming friends any longer, will you please just take her out of my mind once and for? Lord, only you know why that one day, she sashayed into the room, taking my breath away, leaving me speechless."

Once again I have walked so far along the oceanfront that the sun has started its descent to close out another beautiful day. I take a seat here and just watch the sun begin to set itself down on the ocean. The scenery is unlike anything one can describe; it is so lovely and relaxing here right now. I feel as if all my thoughts and troubles are going down with the sun as it goes down into the ocean.

TIME ALONE

must have fallen into a deep sleep out here by the ocean. Now I see only a small part of the moon that is shining tonight, and as for the stars they, themselves are bright and beautiful as they ever were, just like her eyes. When I look in to her beautiful baby browns, they hypnotize me, leaving me unable to seeing my way clearly. I now can decide on if I'm going to take him up on his offer and go into the next town to see if I can find the yellow and red roses. Now as far the note that I will be sending with the flowers goes, I have written it repeatedly, trying to get it to a place I could feel comfortable with it before sending it to such a lovely wildflower as her. For it within itself must be written in a very special way; it must have a great meaning behind it. For she herself is a very special and beautiful wildflower who is with me on this life journey in search of someone to share my life with. For only she and I will be the ones who know just for sure how the note will truly read in the end and the meaning in which it was written just for her. Once again I find myself going over it in my mind, trying to find the right words to put into this special note. You have read the first one I wrote, but I'm now thinking I can make it sound much better than that one. I must put more of my true feeling into it this time and just see how it will read. Before I write this very special note, I must go and tell him I'm going to take the trip into the next town to look for these items.

NEW TOWN ADVENTURE

As i make my way to see him, I remember a time one morning I was on my way to work, I was riding my motorcycle and my lunch box fell off. Well, you can only imagine what happened next. Yes, I ended up in the ditch, and the bike was upside down on top of me. Thank God, I did not get hurt. I am thinking I should tell him about this before asking him if I can still borrow one of his bikes. I have arrived back at his store.

He asks, "How are you today, young man?"

"I am doing good. Thanks for asking, sir. How are you?" "Oh, I'm doing great, thank you. Now how may I help?"

"Do you remember the time you told me if I would like, you would let me borrow one of your bikes to go into next town and see if could find the items I have been looking for? Does that offer still stand?"

He replied, "Yes, it still stands. Would you like to go today?" "Yes, sir, I would."

But I ask, "Just how to do I get there from here?"

"Well, you go out to the main highway and go left and stay on it. You will get there in about an hour or so." He asks, "So you are going take the chance and see if it will work out the two of you?"

"Well, I have been praying about it. I am not sure if she is the one. We're just going to wait and see, for only time will tell."

Now I'm on my way to find these items in the next town. I do find them. Now I must come up with the right words to put in the note.

SECOND NOTE IS WRITTEN

"I would like to show you my thanks and humble gratitude for you taking the time out of your very busy schedule to read a small part of what I had writing. I know you have very little free time for yourself. The yellow rose that is before you represents what may be the beginning of a beautiful and long-lasting friendship. The red rose represents just how one would feel toward their friendship. The baby's breath around them represents the breath of life for their friendship. The greenery among them represents mother earth. The red and yellow bow holds their friendships together. White dots rep-resents the purity of one's relationship. The vase represents the body in which their friendship will grow. Only you know, only you hold the answer. Will their friendship grow, or will it become like unto the waves of the ocean? They come in, and they go out, unto where no one know for certain. I only know God holds the only key to the door of your heart. Only you can open the door of your only heart from within to become a friend to whom of your only choosing. A little difficult with an attitude when need be."

Oh, I feel like I'm forgetting something here now. Could it just be steak and lobster, or could it just be something as simple chicken nuggets? I have no clue, as one might say.

Now the note has been written for the second time from within the depths of my heart. I read it over. I'm not sure if it going to have right effect on such a special lady as her. I'm beginning to feel that the sweet lovely dream was not directly meant for her, but I'm going to go ahead and present them to her just the same to see what her reaction is going to be. For the day has come for the ship to depart back out upon the open sea. Will we be on it together, or will it just be me once again all alone, starting a new journey upon the open sea, where the waves come and they go, out unto, where no one knows just for certain. Just like the day she came sashays into the room, that one morning taking my breath away, for her beauty along outshines all other wildflowers.

ABOUT THE AUTHOR

Clay Mills is a first time author. He fell in love writing when he was very young writing poems. He would write the short poems, and this emerged in the fact that he loved keeping up with his friends via social media. One day, in answering a friend in a conversation which that evolved into complete page. Clay began adding to this paragraph and forming a story line. Once this story line began taking shape, he continued and produced this work.

Clay has two grown children and is blessed with one grandchild. He grow up in a small town in the south United States. He is surrounded with very supportive friends encouraging him to continue pursuing his passion of writing. With this, Clay thanks each and every one who reads his work from the bottom of his heart. May the Lord our God bless you as he has the one who has written this book.

www.ingramcontent.com/pod-product-compliance
Lightning Source LLC
Chambersburg PA
CBHW020320130626
46549CB00003B/946